# Traveler Between Worlds

By

## JO PATTI MUNISTERI

We cannot live
in a world that is not our own
in a world
that is interpreted for us
by others.
An interpreted world
is not a home.
Part of the terror
is to take back
our own listening
to use our own voice
to see our own light.

Saint Hildegard of Bingen
1098—1179

# Table of Contents

Dedication . . . . . . . . . . . . . vii

Preface . . . . . . . . . . . . . . ix

1. Medicines. USA & Australia . . . . . . . . . . .1

2. Vets. Mexico & USA. . . . . . . . . . . . 33

3. Moose & Mukluks. Iraq & Alaska. . . . . . . . 61

4. TCM, Tunji and Master Li. New Zealand & USA . . .93

5. The Shaolin. China . . . . . . . . . . .113

6. Buddhist Smiles. Thailand . . . . . . . . .141

7. Yun Tai Encore. China. . . . . . . . . .159

8. Zumba in Ankawa. Kurdistan, Iraq . . . . . . . .191

9. Daphne's Ghost. Malta . . . . . . . . . 221

10. The Druze. Israel. . . . . . . . . . . 239

11. Shala on HKIA. Afghanistan . . . . . . . . . 259

12. Sequoia in the Mountains. Nepal. . . . . . . . 305

13. Wi Wanyang Wacipi. USA. . . . . . . . . . 329

Photo, Credit . . . . . . . . . . . 353

Acknowledgements . . . . . . . . . 354

# *Dedication*

In memory of Adejola Musa **Olatunji**, martial artist and founder of the New Zealand School of Acupuncture and Traditional Chinese Medicine. Born in Brooklyn, New York USA on April 27, 1950. He died in Wellington, New Zealand on October 12, 2017.

Special thanks to those gifted healers without whom I would not still be alive to write this book. **Dr. Xiaotian Shen** and **Dr. Rosanne Butera**.

With gratitude to **VETS**-*Veterans Exploring Treatment Solutions* for giving me a grant, another experience in another country with plant medicines, and for supporting a community dedicated to helping those wounded by trauma.

To all those who have supported my ideas and work over the years especially my cousin Lori and Aunt Diane; I felt your love across land, sea and sky. Grazie mille.

# *Preface*

People often ask me,

"Why did you write a book?"

My simple answer is,

"Because I have something to say."

Yet upon reflection it is more. I wrote this book to record from a first-hand point of view, the training and advice I received from elders of certain Indigenous tribes and traditions in different parts of our world. To present existing healing modalities which are effective for treating the mind, body and spirit. To share my experience participating in a program hosted by *Veterans Exploring Treatment Solutions* (VETS) supporting recovery from trauma using plant and animal 'medicines'. And to describe a different type of 'travel' which transcends the restrictions of human made national boundaries.

There is a threshold which most do not see nor cross during their life on Earth. Since we have records in drawings, poems, histories, ceremonies and music-we know there are different ways to navigate to and through these spaces which go beyond time and geolocation. We are able to travel between portals of space and time. Between worlds.

The path to these portals requires special abilities which are sometimes passed on as gifts or talents in bloodlines. They may be revealed after extreme trauma or after ingesting specific plant and animal 'medicines'.

Precise rituals taught via human-to-human transmission over thousands of years may also endow a human being these capabilities of 'travel'. The ceremonies and rituals are demanding. They involve strict discipline over mind, body and spirit to be effectual. They take time and years of training from another who has these abilities.

There are very few human beings remaining on Earth who know how to teach and conduct these ceremonies, rituals and quests. With the arrival and acceleration of technologies which track, surveil and disrupt nature and human beings; actual practitioners strive to remain private and off the grid. These elders, 'clever' men and women, medicine people, shamans need to be careful whom they trust and whom they train.

Crossing the portals can also be induced with substances from plants and animals known to be 'medicines'. They can push the mind, spirit and body through the portals with varying degrees of strength.

In fact, recently the biological chemistry of these medicines can be recreated in labs, but in doing so I believe some element of the essence and spirit of that plant and/or animal is lost.

It is a complex issue concerning the purity of medicines and the concurrent need to sustain the flora and fauna populations which possess these properties needed to hallucinate, anaesthetize and propel a human spirit and body to other dimensions.

We will not know the consequences of using these reproduced hallucinogenic medicines for years to come. Be mindful and cautious if you care to use these substances to travel between worlds. Research the credibility of who will be guiding you.

My life path has taken me across diverse landscapes and intertwined with people of all ages, from a number of different cultures and backgrounds. The most powerful guidance I received from elders, Shifus, and extraordinary healers was transmitted in person. Most of these healers are no longer living on Earth. This book shares some of their words and actions I witnessed first-hand.

# CHAPTER ONE

## Medicines

Since I was young, my elder Sicilian aunts, especially my great aunt Jo (Josephine Pino Munisteri) showed me how to use natural ingredients for cooking and for making medicines. Even home-made alcoholic drinks could be used as medicines. She was also an excellent cook. After her only child and husband died, she lived in and managed an apartment building in the Williamsburg section of Brooklyn. Great aunt Jo was also a founding member of the seamstress union in the 1960s. She marched in protests against the appalling conditions in sweatshops. When I was a girl, I was in awe of her.

In my twenties, I moved to Little Italy in New York City. I saw her frequently, since she was often with her brother, (my grandfather) and my grandmother, in Bay Ridge, Brooklyn. I loved and respected them and visited as often as I could. Their affection and support were 'good medicine' to me while I was growing into adulthood.

By that time, I had been exposed to other types of 'medicines' while at Georgetown University (GU). I never confided in my family the other medicines I knew about. They would never have imagined that at a Jesuit run college illegal substances would be so readily available on campus. I know I was surprised to learn how prevalent they were.

While working at the university radio station, and with the GU debate team, drugs were easy to come by. They were popped as pills for staying awake, for sleeping, for partying, or harvested from plants to smoke or bake.

There was always a 'candy man' around to give a taste to newcomers or sell to students. He seemed to appear at parties and at the radio station around exam time. This was the Vietnam War era. The draft was in effect. Deferments for university study depended upon receiving passing grades.

One of the few female seniors at the Foreign Service school warned me at the first party I attended, not to take my eyes off any drink poured and offered.

"Watch out. Sometimes they spike the drinks. Especially for the new girls who don't suspect. They do it if you put your drink down...while you're dancing. And be careful of the older guys who come over and ask you questions but never seem to answer yours. Most likely they are the 'seekers,'" she said.

"What do you mean 'seekers,' Meg?" I asked.

"They are searching for possible recruits. Company men. CIA. Really most of the time you can spot them a mile away once you know what to look for."

"How do you know?"

"They've been working on recruiting my roommate. She speaks three languages fluently, she's smart and she's attractive. She's also naïve."

At the time, I didn't realize that some of us were being 'handled' and guided to parties and gatherings where psychedelics were offered. These guys were observing us and not participating. They hung around campus but we didn't know if they were students. When we tried to find out more about them by asking questions, they were experts at changing the subject. I heard rumors about CIA recruitment tactics. Meg was confirming them.

"I don't want to work for the CIA. I'd rather work for State. That's what they're preparing us for...right?"

"Both organizations have their limitations for gals like us. They use you and then throw you away. Just be careful. Sometimes they double team you, one guy distracts you while the other searches your purse or slips drugs in your drink. They compromise you. Then you're hooked."

"Is that why we get invited to these parties?"

"Starting to catch on, Jo?"

"Here, take this and your eyes will be opened but on our own terms." She offered me a paper with colored squares.

"It looks like paper with colored spots like dot candy," I said.

"It's not candy but it will let you see colors. It's called 'window pane' because it opens windows in your brain. It lasts about eight hours. We have all Sunday to come down before the week starts. Go ahead."

"Are you the candy man tonight then?"

Meg laughed and continued.

"I'll go first so we can trip together. The only way to explain what these drugs do is for you to test it yourself. I promise I'll be with you the whole time. Don't drink any alcohol though. Stick to tonic water. Ready?"

Meg ate a small, light purple square from the paper. She tore off another square for me and told me to open my mouth.

Meg was one of the most sensible and logical people I knew. She wasn't normally a risk taker.

"Open up. We are in for a ride." Meg declared.

I trusted her, so I complied.

The music was pounding all around us. Rock n roll in the 1970s was energetic. I loved to dance.

Meg was smiling at me. My teeth started to feel sensitized and metallic. I felt I couldn't move my mouth to smile back.

As I was dancing, I noticed everyone around me had colors swirling about them. I could see the music. My body was sweating, and I had a strong urge to go outside. My limbs seemed to grow and extend in front of me. I felt like a young colt, unsteady on my new long legs.

I tried to shout to Meg over the music but nothing would come out of my mouth. I pointed to the door to go outside. Meg kept smiling at me like the Cheshire cat. I headed for the door.

Outside, the streetlights looked like crystal prisms. I was enveloped by color. People's faces looked distorted. I tried not to focus on people but on trees and the ground. I felt giddy.

Meg and I walked up stone steps to the main campus. The gothic-like gargoyles on the buildings appeared to have come to life. I saw phantoms on the main lawn and faces in the bonfires up on the hill. It was both exhilarating and terrifying.

Hours later we decided to take a bus to downtown D.C. in the early hours of Sunday. Few people were up yet. We hardly spoke but gaped at the miles of buildings, streets, parked cars, and zombie-like people walking.

We stepped down off the front of the bus after going the full route around D.C. We walked back to campus. I was exhausted, but Meg stayed with me until I slept through the afternoon. We shared dinner together.

"How was it for you?" Meg inquired, sipping a milkshake between speaking.

"Weird, colorful, scary. I don't know if this will last but I had the strongest feeling that I shouldn't work for the government. That all of DC is not a place I should be much longer. I saw scenes of a desert. I saw scenes from a poetry book I read as a child."

"You received a message. From another world. You're lucky."

"Lucky? It wasn't real. I mean I think it wasn't real. I don't know yet."

"This is your first time taking a psychedelic. Not everyone gets messages their first time."

"How many times have you tripped?"

"Just a few times. Mostly with other people, a group of people. Just in case I have a bad trip. I've also learned to guide my own trip once I got used to the jolt into the nether worlds."

"Far out." I gulped.

"Far in." Meg grinned. She took out rolling paper and a bag of what looked like grass. She rolled a joint and lit it. "Here, try some weed. It will bring you down slowly."

"No thanks, Meg I don't smoke."

"Neither do I, but this is medicine. You need it to complete this journey."

"Alright, just this once." I inhaled and coughed.

"That's what they all say," Meg teased.

I did feel more relaxed and the buzzing sensation in my head ceased. But the taste in my mouth was not pleasant.

"No, really. One time is enough for me."

I was careful to be in control of my body, and what I put in my body. While some of my friends enjoyed 'tripping', I didn't.

That was my introduction to plant medicine and psychedelics. The messages stayed with me and my third eye was opened again.

I say again, because as a child enduring trauma and abuse, I had already experienced a thrust into other worlds. But over time I had shut down what my inner eyes saw after those experiences. It was too painful while I lived at home to examine or relive the events that led to my excarnation and travel on other planes of existence.

The first time I distinctly remember jumping out of my physical body was when I was four years old. We were living in Ontario, Canada at the time. I attended a Catholic kindergarten close by our house. Each day I walked there and back with some neighborhood children.

It was winter. After a heavy snowfall, one of the older boys brought a toboggan out so we could ride down the makeshift fleecy white hills. I was placed at the back and enjoyed falling off and getting back on, being covered in snow and making snow angels. My whole-body snow suit was soaked by the time I got home.

My mother was usually taking a nap when I came home from school. She was pregnant with her fourth child. We had recently moved from California to Canada. She was moody with a violent temper. I didn't want to disturb her so I crept downstairs to the basement where the furnace was placed.

Carefully I peeled off all my wet clothes and put them on top of the furnace. I was standing near it waiting for my clothes to dry, when I heard my mother's footsteps. I thought I would hide but I couldn't find a place fast enough as she came down the steps.

She looked around and started yelling at me, asking what happened and why my clothes were wet? My mother didn't let me answer but started hitting me. I fell down on the concrete. I was terrified.

My mother continued beating me and shouting at me as I lay naked on the concrete basement floor. The pain caused me to see outside myself. I could no longer feel my body. She told me to go upstairs and get dressed and to "Get out of my sight!"

I remember trying to stop crying as I ran upstairs. By the time I started dressing I had come back into my body. It was a jolting sensation. I felt hurt, pain all over.

At school in Canada, I would sometimes still wet my pants. Actually, I displayed many signs which, to an educated observer or teacher, indicated I was being abused. But in the 1950s, this wasn't ever spoken about.

To make matters worse, each time I had an 'accident' I had to sit behind the curtain on the stage in the school gym and wait for my underwear to dry. They put it on the heaters in view of everyone. It was mortifying. I developed a stutter and a lisp during my time at that school.

After this happened a few times, the teacher called a priest to come talk to me. He came while I was behind the curtain sitting without underwear in my little school dress. He was definitely a predator. He would ask to "feel and make sure you are dry" and spread my legs to "pat me" before I could return to class. The priest told me that "This was our special secret with God" and soon I would be able to come see him when I learned how "to control myself."

When I tried to tell my mother, I didn't want to go to school because I was afraid of the priest, she shouted, "You're lying.

You're just a lazy, stupid, good-for-nothing who doesn't want to go to school!" I wasn't even five years old.

Author at three years old on tricycle in Concord, California

By the time I was seven, I could almost will myself to 'jump out' of my body and soar to the ceiling to view myself from above.

Throughout my early life, certain events or situations would trigger this same excarnating sensation, and I would have to will myself to re-enter my body. Once I was back in, there would be a slight delay. Then I would feel the physical and psychic pain seize me. I would be filled with anxiety. Over time I learned to disguise my nervousness and internalize my pain.

While at Georgetown, I was selected to be part of the first Psycho Cybernetics course and a subject for hypnosis with Head of GU's psychology department, Dr. Arnold Mysior. He trained me to use my ability to disassociate and 'travel' without the use of any medicines. Dr. Mysior taught me to use my own powers of concentration.

He also taught me how to compartmentalize information and memories so they wouldn't be intrusive. This involved daily journaling, visualizing, dream interpretation, dream inceptions, and weekly hypnosis sessions at the Georgetown Department of Psychology in Healy basement.

Later, I unraveled painful parts of my childhood and interpreted dreams and messages from my unconscious with Dr. Charles Socarides.

Dr. Socarides was a good friend and a Harvard colleague of my paternal aunt Lauradele Patti Munisteri. As a psychiatrist, he helped hundreds if not thousands of patients over his long career. He was successful in helping those who had experienced sexual abuse in childhood, more specifically at the hands of an abuser of the same gender. He used a combination of Freudian and Jungian analysis, and psychotherapy techniques.

My aunt Lauradele told him of my situation as well as the background she knew. Dr. Socarides agreed to take me as a patient while I was a student at Circle-in-the-Square Performing Arts School in New York City in 1978.

Dr. Socarides interviewed my father in person, and my mother over the phone. She refused to meet him and denigrated his methods. Yet she kept calling him to ask what I was saying, and ask "What was wrong with me?" Doctor Socarides was able to gauge a measure of who she was and her pathologies by her responses to his questions.

My mother refused to take any responsibility for her abusive behavior toward me, in fact she blamed me (a child) for "making her lose her temper" and accused me of lying, yet admitted to a few incidents that revealed some of her dark beliefs and behavior.

My father believed what Dr. Socarides and I recounted, but his answer to the pain and abuse I suffered was,

"There isn't anything I can do now. It's over. I'm paying for Dr. Socarides to help you. That's enough."

Dr. Charles Socarides MD, in New York, 1970s

Only after decades, and just before his death did my father finally apologize for not protecting me earlier in my life. My mother never did. She left this world unrepentant.

It is important to understand that most children who have been moderately to severely abused during their childhood have a greater potential to adapt using compartmentalization and dissociation. They often become hypervigilant. Their senses are heightened to alert them to possible harm. Our neural pathways are changed because of these imprinting experiences.

Unfortunately, there are individuals, groups and organizations that recognize and seek out victims of trauma who have been wounded and/or desensitized in these ways. They use them for their own purposes and prey upon their vulnerabilities for their own power, or for their perverse cruelty.

On the other hand, a person with these different abilities once they are recognized, can help identify others who have been traumatized and/or those who are the predators and criminals. They have a developed instinct and seventh sense for detecting perpetrators.

There are a few professions which attract and even embrace those who have had troubled childhoods and survived trauma. The performing arts, the military, as well as criminal networks are the most significant.

Over my lifetime, I've had experience with all three of the above-mentioned sectors of society. I expand on these experiences in this and my first non-fiction book, *Traveling Off the X*.

When I was working and living in New York City in the 1980s, my friend and fellow performing artist Jo Anderson, introduced me to a healer from North Carolina. Her name was Katherine Leonard. She was a Tsalagi or Cherokee elder woman who had the gift of 'sight'. Jo thought she could help me refine my abilities for use in my work and to heal the relationships with some of my family members. I had a large family.

Katherine conducted workshops for females only, which were essentially for overcoming fears and preparing for motherhood. She had helped many women recover from post trauma reactions, from violence and abuse. Her small groups of five or six women met in a rented apartment in Manhattan. Every day she smudged it with sage and cedar. You could smell the potent and invigorating plant medicines before you knocked on her door.

Upon entrance, I noticed that instead of chairs or couches in her living room, she had carpets and large throw pillows arranged in a circle on the floor. An assortment of different size hand drums stood in one corner. Candles and low lights illuminated her home.

As was her protocol, Katherine initially held a private session with me before deciding if I was a suitable candidate for her group sessions. She spoke to me about my grandmothers, my mother, my sister, my aunts, the strong female figures throughout my life. She spoke accurately about some exact phrases they had used with me, and of events that had happened when I was younger. She asked me to identify my fears and my strengths. Then she invited me to consider joining a healing circle with other women.

She held these workshops for three hours at night, twice a week for a month. Our tasks included meditation and prayer, visualizations, speaking about what we experienced, and homework to improve our awareness of our environment, and our thoughts.

As an example, one task she assigned to me was to look at the shadows of people and articulate what I saw. This was a fascinating mission. I walked the streets of the city finding people's shadows on sunny days and becoming aware of their shadows in all weather.

"Learn to see light in the dark," she coached me. "Your mother was a very dark teacher. You had a visceral experience of darkness. You know how to sense it, if you will trust your instincts."

Toward the end of the month, Katherine asked us to go to a crime scene where a young woman was recently raped and murdered. There were no suspects yet for these crimes. There was no police tape at the scene. I assumed law enforcement and detectives had already been there and left. Katherine had the key.

We went through the apartment and up to the roof in silence. I believe we all felt our spines tingling as soon as we arrived. Katherine instructed us to be still and 'feel' and 'see' the energies still lingering in the spaces as we walked through. She tutored us in further observations with all our senses-our sense of time, of color, of proxemics, of movement, of shapes, of the presence of others, in addition to the senses of smell, sight, taste, touch and hearing. We retraced our steps and walked back to her place. We discussed what we each observed.

"Remember what you saw and felt," Katherine instructed. "Energies are often around a crime like that one. She is between worlds until her spirit is released. Her spirit is trying to reach others to cry out what happened. To unveil this predator. A rapist. Her killer."

While riding the subways home late that night, I felt more situationally aware. This was in the days before Rudy Giuliani was mayor of New York City and he vigorously battled crime. As Jo remarked, "New York is bootcamp for life."

My last session with Katherine and our group involved a deep meditation and visualization regarding our mothers and death. I saw myself dancing to the music from the *Wizard of Oz* at the end of my meditation. The song playing in my mind was "Ding, dong, the witch is dead."

Afterwards, we drank sage tea. I felt uplifted and stronger.

\* \* \*

In New York in the 1970s, the American Indian Movement (AIM) launched a peaceful protest at Ellis Island, the gate for millions of immigrants coming into the United States, including my own family from Italy. Russell Means, an Oglala Lakota Sioux, was one of their main leaders. The buildings on the island had been closed since the 1950s, and were in poor condition. This was to be a symbolic act by AIM similar to their protest at Alcatraz on the west coast.

Later on in the 1980s, a number of AIM leaders and members from different tribes passed through their ad hoc offices in New York City. New York City and surrounding boroughs hosted hundreds of activists between the 1960s and the 1990s.

Russell Means testified before the US Senate on January 30, 1989, explaining to them about the economic hardship caused by living on reservations and "assimilation policies" which were designed to fail. He pointed out the corruption and graft in the Bureau of Indian Affairs (BIA) since its establishment in 1824. Native Americans were not given the right to vote in Federal elections until 1824. Arizona, New Mexico only granted voting rights in 1948. Montana, North Dakota and South Dakota did not have voting facilities for tribal communities until the 1980s.

AIM advocated for repeal of Federal laws restricting religious and civil rights that had been instituted against Native Americans since the 1800s. These laws forbid sacred ceremonies including the Sun Dance, called *Wi Wanyang Wacipi* in the Lakota language. I learned a little about these ceremonies from Katherine and from other Native Americans I met in New York City in the 1980s.

Later, when I was called to be a Sundancer in dreams and inipi, I consulted personally with Lakota elders. They trained me (there is no comparable English word for the years of apprenticeship and learning you undergo for the Wi Wanyang Wacipi ceremonies). Chief Archie Fire Lame Deer was my lekshi (uncle in Lakota) and guide for the Sun Dance. His way *did not include peyote or plant medicines that contained hallucinogenic properties.*

Lekshi Archie Fire believed we could reach those portals by fasting, prayer and inipi (sweat lodge).He taught us these rituals, and the steps of the Sun Dance to the chants, drumbeats and earth rhythms over days and nights, months and years of preparation. He traveled to Europe and Australia seeking to share his knowledge before he passed away.

I began my journey in becoming a Sundancer years before I met my husband, Marty Schmidt, but I had to pause during the years our two children, Denali and Sequoia, were very young. They needed my full attention, especially since their father was gone six to eight months a year doing mountain guiding and pursuing extreme sports.

For the most part, Marty was not interested in my work or spiritual path. However, in 1995, he came down with Dengue fever. His joints were like he was 100 years old. He was in pain and could not work for months, all while we were trying to finish building our house and gardens in rural Australia. The nearest doctor in Bellingen told us it would probably take a year or more for him to recover. At the same time, I had symptoms of Parkinson's disease and was diagnosed as such, with no known cure in western medicine. We were at a low point and terribly worried about our children and the future.

We lived with three other families sharing 5 hectares each, bordering a national forest. We were off the main grid and installed solar power panels for electricity. We had a diesel pump to pipe in water from a river which bordered our

Gumbaynggirr elders Auntie Phoebe, author and Auntie
Jessie in 1996, New South Wales, Australia.
Photo by elder Auntie Tresna.

property. Three of the Aboriginal elders I worked with came out to visit us and see what was wrong. One of them was a gifted healer we knew as Auntie Jessie. The others were Auntie Phoebe and Auntie Bea.

Auntie Jessie took me outside under one of our large Eucalyptus trees. She held my hand and told me:

"One of the clever men from your own country is coming here. I can do part of a healing for you and your husband, but he will help you with the rest. You need to listen to what he has to say."

"Who is coming here, Auntie Jess? I don't know of anyone," I replied.

"He's coming. He's coming soon," she assured me.

She walked about the outside of our house saying prayers while my children watched in quiet respect. The other aunties had tried to speak with Marty. They came out with stern looks on their faces.

"We will talk to Uncle Ken. Maybe he can come out to speak to Marty."

We all hugged goodbye with my whole body continuing to shake uncontrollably. It was hard to believe someone from the USA was coming to this faraway, rural place in Australia.

Yet only two months later I received word that Chief Archie Fire Lame Deer and his daughter Josephine were coming to Australia and they wanted to come up the coast to where we were. I was asked if we could host them at our home for a few days. We were honored they would be staying with us.

News spread quickly by word of mouth. By the time they arrived, men from all parts of the Thora valley came to help build the sweat lodge and listen to Chief Archie Fire Lame Deer. I hadn't known there were Maori in the valley, as well as Bidayuh from Malaysia, and a few Germans living there also. All of them came to participate.

We found a large spot near the river where we could construct the lodge and yet have privacy for everyone. We made two separate lodges. Chief Archie directed preparations for the men and boys lodge, and Josephine directed them for women and girls. Gumbaynggirr men, boys, girls and women arrived to participate. The ceremonies and talks went on over three days.

Praying was fervent and constant. Many came for healing and clarity. Marty improved visibly after the second inipi (sweat lodge). So, did I. At one point, Chief Archie and Gumbaynggirr elder Ken Walker spoke together, then rejoined the larger group.

Uncle Ken Walker came over to me.

"We all have our crosses to bear," he said somewhat cryptically. "Be prepared to do what is asked of you...for all of us."

I nodded but was not clear about what he meant at the time.

Denali, Sequoia and the other children swam in the river after the lodges. We ate a combined potluck meal and made a fire further up on the bank. It was the one- and only-time people from all over the valley had come together.

It was on the last day of these ceremonies performed in rural New South Wales, Australia, I made the vow to Sundance for four years. Now I had two personal reasons to commit. One, in gratitude for my healing and that of my family members, and two, in accord with my Aboriginal family to seek answers about the many Bundjalung and Dunghutti children who were taken away, stolen and never heard from again.

Until the 1970s, it was legal for Australian government agencies to remove Aboriginal children and make them wards of the state. These children were kidnapped by government services and hundreds are still missing today. They were known as *The Stolen Generations* in Australia. The wounds from these government policies are still open and festering.

Like the Native Americans in the USA and Canada, Aboriginal Australians were targeted for 'assimilation'. They were not legally able to vote in Australia until 1965. Queensland was the last state to agree.

It wasn't until 1985, that the last legal disparities for citizen rights and responsibilities were equalized for Aboriginal and non-Aboriginal Australians. By then they had lost most of their languages and traditions in the hundred years of attacks against them.

Chief Archie Fire Lame Deer had his own traditional Lakota way of training for those he would bring to Wi Wanyang Wacipi. You must commit to four years, learn all the Lakota traditional songs to conduct, as well as participate in, inipi (sweat lodges). You needed to prepare all your materials including hundreds of tobacco ties for your Hanblecheya (Crying for a Dream or Vision Quest) and learn the ceremonial language included in the Sun Dance ways. You needed to be sincere in your vows.

You must refrain from any criminal behavior, alcohol or illegal drug use in your preparation year, and thereafter. Prayer needs to be a daily habit, as does remembering your dreams which are often signs or messages. As often as possible, you were to participate in inipis. You needed to take care of your Chanupa (pipe) and use sacred sage and cedar for smudging, as plant medicines. Becoming a sundancer also required a sacrifice of time and money to travel back to the States for Sun Dance each Northern Hemisphere summer for two weeks, but I managed.

It was understood you did not speak (or write) about your personal experience, messages or feelings during ceremony. These were for you, your elders, medicine men, your family, and maybe your tribe for the time that they took place. They were between you and God (Tunkashila) and not for public display. These rules/ guidelines are just a few examples of the 'requirements' to be a sundancer.

There are more instructions and teachings you can find in literature written about the Sun Dance and the Sioux by those from Lakota/Dakota trib-

Lakota Chief Archie Fire Lame Deer. 1935–2001.
Photo by Richard Erdoes

al families. People even post online and on social media pages about their Sun Dances. This is something the elders that taught me would have frowned upon, or even forbidden. But those Wicasca Wakan (Medicine men) who taught me have passed on to the Spirit World.

In the days before social media and surveillance, no cameras, recording equipment, or cellphones were permitted on Crow Dog's Paradise, Ironwood, or other Sun Dance grounds that I knew. There were guards at the entrance and exits. They checked all cars and vehicles coming in, opening up trunks, glove compartments and sometimes personal bags.

The only photos permitted for publications before 2000, were those authorized by Chief Frank Fools Crow, Chief Archie Fire and Chief Leonard Emanual Crow Dog Sr. Mr. Richard Erdoes, from Austria, was given permission to photograph and write books about these men and women, the Lakota ceremonies, and their life stories. You may read more authentic information in his books *The Sun Dance People, Lame Deer Seeker of Visions, Lakota Woman, Crying for a Dream, Gift of Power, Crow Dog-Four Generations of Medicine Men,* as well as others he wrote before his death in Santa Fe, New Mexico, in 2008.

Most people are not aware that Native American or 'Indian' religious ceremonies were outlawed in the USA until the late 1970s. The American Indian Religious Freedom Act of 1978 (AIRFA) (42 U.S.C. § 1996.) protects the rights of Native Americans to exercise their traditional religions by ensuring access to sites, use and possession of sacred objects, and the freedom to worship through ceremonial and traditional rites.

Prior to implementation of this legislation, tribal members and supporters were arrested and imprisoned if they were caught practicing their own religion.

In schools, speaking any language other than English, and especially 'Indian' languages were forbidden. Children were punished severely for not speaking English. Decades of forced separation (essentially kidnapping) of children from their families, servitude in boarding schools or workstations far from their homes, was the sanctioned policy in the USA, Canada and Australia. Children were forced to give up their culture, their family ties, their languages, their traditions and their spiritual practices.

The state governments and various religious institutions enforced these brutal policies. In the United States the First Amendment rights of the Constitution were aggressively denied to Native Americans up until the 1990s. Finally, in 1993, Congress passed the *Religious Restoration Act* after the US Supreme Court case Oregon vs Smith.

The use of plant medicines including peyote, was further protected for the Native American Church and other religious groups with the passage of the American Indian Religious Freedom Act Amendments in 1994.

During a particularly difficult Sundance season in South Dakota in 1997, I was part of the ceremonies with a woman from Canada. She was Cree from Canada, married to a Lakota Brule man. They were members of the Native American Church and used peyote as part of their ceremonies in conjunction with Wi Wanyang Wacipi. They were friends of Leonard Crow Dog and his wife Mary, spiritual leaders of the Native American church living on Rosebud reservation at the time. They introduced me to Leonard at his camp.

Mary and Leonard Crow Dog at Crow Dogs Paradise on Rosebud reservation in South Dakota, USA, 1970s. Photo by Richard Erdoes.

At that phase of my life, I was having a very tough time with my husband. At the same time, I was doing very difficult work with the Indigenous, Aboriginal Studies department at Coffs Harbour TAFE (Technical and Further Education), and with Link Up Aboriginal Corporation. Much of my time was spent in investigations of stolen children from the Gumbaynggirr tribal area. We were compiling evidence to be included in a report to the Australian Parliament on the 'Stolen Generations' titled, "Bringing Them Home".

Leonard Crow Dog spoke in English and Lakota. After Sundance, one of the Poor Bear family, who was with us in our camp at Crow Dog's Paradise, said I should, "Take the medicine", to see clearer.

He arranged for a Native American church ceremony on Pine Ridge reservation. The ceremony was held at night with a small, solemn group in a tipi. We were smudged with sage and cedar before we entered. Everyone sat on blankets spread out on the grass. They used a small water drum to start the prayers and chant-like singing. A bowl with a gritty liquid was passed around. I only took one large sip but others took more.

Time seemed to both stand still and expand in the next hour. I couldn't be sure how long passed before I started to 'enter the medicine'. For me the effects were gradual and mild at first. I saw 'spirits' in the tipi. I felt rushing wind and water all around me. Lightning-like cracks and colors came into my field of vision. The sounds of prayers and music were mesmerizing. I felt my body swaying. This was medicine from the peyote plant.

I closed my eyes since other people's faces were distracting and distorted. I wanted to concentrate. The darkness was soft initially, and then I felt I was falling. I wanted to stop and tried to stand, but someone pushed me down to sit again. I opened my eyes briefly.

Then I saw scenes as if in a film of war. I heard other drums with a martial beat. I heard the words, "Prepare for war!" I may have even shouted these words because the Lakota man next to me handed me the bowl with more medicine and nodded for me to drink.

The hallucinations softened. I heard children playing, saw them running and suddenly again I saw scenes of fire, smoke and explosions. The ceremony went on for hours into the night.

At the end, the Chanupa (sacred pipe) was passed around. We all smudged again. Someone slowly opened the tipi flap. My first journey with peyote opened my mind to the other portals and consciousness that coexist with what is labeled, 'reality'.

Over the next weeks and months, I processed the sights and sounds from that ceremony. I returned to Australia and began to re-prioritize and change my life for my children, my colleagues and myself.

New ideas for our investigations and strategies for reconciliation occurred to me. I shared my experiences with my Aboriginal elders. For them, the 'Dreamtime' was as real as day-to-day time. They didn't need plant medicine to travel between worlds. It seemed to be part of their DNA. They knew how the navigate passages between different registers of consciousness and time. I continually learned from them.

As I studied more about Traditional Chinese Medicine (TCM) and Esoteric Acupuncture in concert with the Lakota ways, diving deeper into the theological writings of Thomas Acquinas, the poetry of Rumi, William Blake and other mystic writers; I came back to the ancient wisdom reminding us, "We are all one. We are all related". In Lakota — *Hau Mitakuye Oyasin*

It is not easy to reach this understanding, especially with all the technologies which absorb our attention, diminish our senses and instincts, and indoctrinate us with materialistic values. People are taught to view medicines as commodities. The individual prescription for health in body, mind and spirit is rare.

Most doctors, religious leaders, psychologists and teachers subscribe to a 'one size fits all' system of diagnostics and categories for treatment. They will take shortcuts to increase their quantity of patients, clients or students. Money is often the overriding motivation. They are impatient for results.

As Dr. Miko Sankey Ph D., L.Ac. points out in the second volume of his book *Esoteric Acupuncture-Discern the Whisper*:

> "Understanding what is being shown to us at the higher levels of consciousness takes time and patience.

A time lock is inherent and always present to some degree in the energy field of each individual. This time lock acts as a safety net to assure that one will not receive information that is too difficult to handle.

Coffs Harbour Indigenous Studies department team.
Author seated back right.
Photo by Beatrice Ballangarry, Australia 1994

Only in certain cases, such as physical accidents, trauma, sudden kundalini rising, or the ingestion of psychedelic drugs or hallucinogenic plants, will a person experience heightened levels of consciousness without having to do prior inner work. In those instances, the periods of heightened awareness are usually hard to sustain and usually hard to reproduce naturally without repeated use of an outside stimulant.

A more natural method of breaking into this time lock requires patience and dedicated meditation, along with the Will-to-Know. The Will-to-Know is the beginning step in one's inward journey. Aging alone doesn't guarantee that we will reach a level of higher consciousness on the Inner Plane".

# CHAPTER TWO

## *Vets*

In the Fall of 2020, after the combination of a serious health crisis in our family, a frustrating work situation, the continuing plandemic restrictions, and the harsh, gray, cold climate of Bethel, Alaska where I was living at the time; I noticed I was experiencing post trauma reactions. My temper was short. Nightmares from different parts of my experiences in Afghanistan, Ukraine and Iraq were disturbing my sleep. I was eating for comfort as I had never done before, and I felt my world was 'closing in' and dark.

After treating patients with post trauma over the years using acupuncture and Traditional Chinese Medicine

(TCM), I finally admitted to myself *I might need help* to navigate the cluster of symptoms. My daughter, Sequoia and her husband, John, were shutting me off and this created a hole in my heart that tore at my core.

I decided to visit them in Idaho for Thanksgiving. I would schedule a counseling session with a therapist in their town of Twin Falls. He came highly recommended by Catholic Relief Services. Felix Arnold specialized in post trauma reactions, mediation and family conflict. He worked with horses for therapy and created a non-profit he called Egala-equestrian assisted psychotherapy. He was a veteran, a career military man in the US Marine Corps. He was a drill instructor and Chief Warrant Officer 3, serving for over twenty-three years. He was a husband and father, earned his Bachelor's degree in Economics, Masters in Social Work, and certificates in different techniques for counseling over his lifetime. I called and made an appointment for us, for two consecutive sessions to start.

When Sequoia agreed to a two-hour session (that I would pay for), I was relieved. But even in the waiting room, she refused to speak to me and kept her eyes on her phone. When Felix came out to meet us, she changed her tone and walked ahead of me into his office.

When we sat down, he asked us what we hoped to accomplish in the session. I had one initial objective. Clarity. Where and why had communication stopped?

Sequoia started getting agitated when he asked more about our family history and my work. As I was recounting about deaths in our family, challenges with having to be overseas, and about my disappointment in Sequoia and John's lack of integrity in financial dealings with them over the year; Sequoia started interrupting.

Felix reminded her it was my time to speak and she would have her chance soon. Then Sequoia started questioning his techniques and his competence as a counselor. She kept raising her voice and said it was a waste of time. Finally, she stood up abruptly and said she was leaving. She said she had her own therapist.

Both Felix and I asked her to please stay and try to talk this out but she stomped out the door. I started to cry. For me, this was unusual in a public setting. Felix handed me a box of tissues. Then he sat at the edge of his chair and looked at me directly.

"First, I want to thank you for your service. I have a good idea of the type of work you've done."

I was astonished. Very few people had ever said these words to me personally. Often there was a general pronouncement in the Joint Operations Center (JOC) or at a conference, or onboard military transport, or in emails. This was just to me. I sighed.

"Second, for some of these issues I recommend you get a good lawyer right away and separate your financial relationship from your parental relationship."

For the next two hours we had an in depth, productive conversation. He asked hard hitting questions and I felt he understood my answers. He gave me an extra hour for us to sort out next steps to try, and his reassurance that I could call him from Alaska, although he didn't do formal counseling over screens or phone.

His manner was straight up, practical and yet heart felt. My way forward was clear even if it would be hard to draw the boundaries with my daughter and son-in-law given the serious health issues he was facing, and the fact Sequoia was my only living child. I loved her so much and missed her company and communication more than ever. But I would have to be stronger if honest and genuine communications were to build between us. There were no excuses anymore for her behavior, stressed as she was by her husband's brush with death, and the deaths of her brother and father (my son and ex-husband) in our family.

Felix walked me to the reception desk and gave me his card.

"You can leave a message anytime. I know the time difference in Alaska. Don't hesitate to call and I will call you back."

We shook hands and I thanked him again. I was beholden to the Catholic Relief Services for the recommendation. I stopped by the Catholic church, Saint Edwards, in the center of Twin Falls before going for a walk atop the majestic gorge looking down at the Snake River. It was the day before Thanksgiving 2020.

Winter was in full force when I returned to Bethel, but I had a plan for 2021 to guide me through the grim weather. This included researching programs for helping those with post trauma *without the use of pharmaceutical drugs.*

Winter in Bethel, Alaska.
Cemetery outside St. Sophia church

There was only one acupuncturist in Bethel, but he was woefully inadequate in Traditional Chinese Medicine (TCM). I did needle myself, but certain points on the back of my body and the interior of my arms were too difficult for me to do. There was no one to exchange treatments with where I would live for the next nine months.

A number of programs were possible for people who had served in the military, or as a contractor for military support, or were or had been the spouse of a special operations veteran, as I was. I started doing research online and reading the emails I received with greater interest and focus.

Meanwhile, to keep my spirits up, I played my flute and wrote. I planned to self-publish my second book of poetry, and I was invited to be a contributing writer for Communities Digital News (CDN), an online political news platform.

In my free time I immersed myself in researching and writing about current geopolitical situations I knew about from living and working in those countries. I was already a contributing writer for other sites including *Small Wars Journal.*

I wrote an article a week for CDN. Submerging myself in my writing reminded me of the accomplishments and positive experiences I had. It also helped me keep a wider focus since I felt the walls, the dark, the isolation and job frustration narrowed my view. The Lower Kuskokwin School District (LKSD) ROTC Sargeant told me with deep sorrow, that in the first year of the restrictions due to Covid, six high school aged students committed suicide. Some boys just went out on the tundra and 'fell asleep'. This was registered as death by exposure.

The longer project was to write my non-fiction book. This would be my purpose besides work with the school district, which was slogging along.

Both Felix Arnold and my TCM doctor in Texas, Dr. Xiaotian Shen, encouraged me to keep writing. This advice echoed what my mentor for article writing, USMC David Dilegge, said. He had told me just before he died in May 2020,

"Keep writing!" I kept his words in mind. They sustained me.

Dave founded the *Small Wars Journal* with publisher Bill Nagle. When he retired from the USMC as a counterintelligence and human intelligence (HUMINT) officer, he went on to work as a contractor, civilian analyst and trainer. He was self-taught on computers and desktop publishing. He created multiple websites and was a fellow 'paisano' having both Italian and Scottish ancestry. I was honored to know him in the last years of his life though we never met in person. We would speak briefly by phone and mostly via emails. He cut straight to the chase, always, but with a sense of humor and a thirst for the truth. He was a rigorous taskmaster.

The working title for my non-fiction book would be "Traveling Off the X". I sent query letters to independent publishers I thought would be interested. This time, I would not ask my daughter if her company would publish my book as they did my first poetry book, *Kismet*. It would be part of my promise to separate business dealings from family dealings...if at all possible.

My first choice, Defiance Press out of Conroe, Texas, accepted my manuscript in early 2021. We entered into a contract. I was satisfied with their terms and their editors.

This project partially filled the void in my personal life, at least for a while. I struggled to keep a positive outlook.

My birthday was in March. My daughter didn't even send a text. I could see from her social media accounts she was celebrating birthdays of her recent clients and their families. It hurt, but I persevered, occupying myself with work, my book, compulsory professional development courses for LKSD, as well as new skills I was learning. But the nightmares continued.

After Easter, I decided to call Felix Arnold to set up another counseling session for late May 2021, when I would have some time off. I called the Crosspointe Center in Twin Falls, Idaho on May 7.

"I'm so sorry, but Felix Arnold passed away two days ago."

My stomach felt as if it had been punched. I found out after inquiring further, that Felix had taken the Covid 'vaccine' and died suddenly. His death (like so many) was labeled vaguely, "Covid related". Most people working in clinics were required to 'take the vaccine', an experimental medical injection, when it became available. They could lose their jobs or clinical practice privileges if they didn't. I wondered if that was the case with Felix. I said a silent prayer for him. His listening and counsel had changed my life already, even after such a brief encounter. Sometimes one deep conversation about important issues can change your life direction. I was grateful but also sorry. I would miss him, as would many others.

Providentially, I heard about a 'plant medicine' therapy that was tested over five years with veterans. It was not yet legal in the USA, therefore those selected had to travel to Mexico, but they had a number of grants to support those who could not afford the treatment or the travel. I wrote them an inquiring email. I listed some of my

Felix Michael Arnold
1955–2021

work, my former marriage to a USAF PJ, the deaths in our family and my symptoms. I was sent a long application form.

My hesitation in filling in the form was due to a new job I had been offered which was to start in Abu Dis, Jerusalem, Israel in August 2021. I declined another year with LKSD for a multitude of reasons. The new contract I'd been offered was through Bard College in New York, but sponsored by USAID and other sources. I would be director for new curriculum design and evaluation in a multinational, multi university team including Al Quds university as the base, the American University of Central Asia (AUCA) in Bishkek, Kyrgyzstan, and Arizona State University in Phoenix, Arizona.

It sounded like a conscionable job more suited to my skills and experience. I needed a change. However, my priority was my health and this new position would most likely be stressful. I was not able to choose my team, it was chosen for me. I could tell the Dean I was to report to at Abu Dis Bard College in Jerusalem was a difficult personality. I heard the temporary Dean at AUCA was similar.

Nevertheless, I signed the contract in June 2021, and concurrently sent off my application to two veteran run programs in the US. Veterans Exploring Treatment Solutions or VETS. They had bases in Texas, California and Mexico. The Mighty Oaks Foundation was based in California and used other techniques. Neither responded right away after I filled in their questionnaires. I had no choice but to be patient and continue with my plans. Meanwhile my intrusive memories besieged me.

My vacation time was coming up from LKSD. I needed to get away. A pet sitting opportunity for a US Army vet in Denver presented itself. I accepted and serendipitously she had just returned from doing plant medicine treatment for PTSD in Costa Rica. She told me of other veterans who benefitted from this type of journey.

We spoke in depth about her experience and she gave me the name of the supervising directors and the location in case I wanted to contact them. We went on a hike in the hills outside Denver, I swam in the apartment pool, and had a great furry cat for company. All these eased my mind and body. I felt ready to begin a new job.

Al Quds Bard was supposed to send me my ticket to Tel Aviv in August 2021, although the restrictions due to

COVID meant much of our collegial work and interaction with students would be at best hybrid, meaning part remote and part in-person work or contact.

Our team included one Palestinian woman, one Palestinian man, three American men based both in Jerusalem and the States. We had faculty members from ASU, and from AUCA, as well as various specialty faculty and administrators contributing from all four universities. I was facilitating and participating in Zoom meetings at least five times a week. Three of the universities maintained a Monday through Friday schedule, while Al Quds had a Sunday through Thursday schedule. I had three or four different time zones to coordinate. It was rather exhausting.

One of the American men openly expressed that he thought he should have my position. He went about searching online and trying to find 'dirt' on me. These days, that means anything or any association that could be construed to demonstrate prejudice in the woke narrative of the West— such as perceived racism and/or what were considered the wrong political views. He made a formal complaint to the Dean and to HR stating my associations and manner of leadership made him feel he "wasn't in a safe space," along with other accusations. Then he resigned.

At first, I was relieved, and a few of the team expressed similar sentiments, since this individual had not been contributing to our curriculum tasks, and he had personality challenges which held up our timeline for delivering materials.

But then, the Dean decided he would not accept this man's resignation. He said this man was a 'protected minority' since he had recently declared his bisexuality. He would *change my job* description and place of work to accommodate this young man. I could either accept the new terms, lesser pay and benefits, or resign myself.

I didn't have another job lined up, and it was August. Most positions in education were already contracted. I had my arm twisted (as they say) to continue. I signed the new one-year contract and simultaneously realized it was really the Open Society University Network (OSUN) which was controlling the entire project. This was the Soros organization. The education sector was overseen by Alexander Soros, who was good friends with Jonathan Becker and Daniel Terris, the two deans of AUCA and Al Quds Bard, respectively.

Later I discovered ASU is one of the Soros network's largest universities and the second largest university in the United States. The curriculum we were creating, testing and implementing would be on their international data platform. OSUN had a definite slant to all its human rights, literacy and language projects. It is incredibly biased toward communism and anti-Americanism. It would be a tremendous challenge to usher in objectivity in these subjects with this sponsor, but I would try.

It also gave me a chance to look inside this notorious network which had an invasive and pervasive influence in education, the justice and other systems in much of the world. I had dealt with them while working in Armenia (2008-2010) where they sponsored the Salzburg International Medical Conference slots our residents and doctors attended. It had grown significantly since then.

Ultimately this meant I would now be based in the USA, performing the vast majority of my work and coordinating online. This was extremely disappointing but some of my international team members were keen to make it work. They helped lift my morale. I forged on. We would have to get permission for travel. For most of my contract, the teams from other countries would come to ASU. I would not travel out till later.

My base would be in Texas. Luckily, I found a US Army veteran family looking for a long-term house and pet sitter for their Dogo Argentino. That would work for me, and I could look for a more permanent base once I was back in America. I had been working and living overseas for the most part since 2005. Time to settle. I bought a beater car, too.

At the beginning of 2022, I received word back from VETS. We set up a phone call with the man who oversaw/directed all treatment in Mexico. He was originally from Canada. He wasn't a US military veteran but he had experience with plant medicines. He already had an organization for retreats and healing that cooperated with and became part of VETS over the years, from what I understood. His name was Trevor. We had a long conversation and got on well. It seemed we were on the same wavelength.

Trevor asked what dates would be possible for me to spend about a week in Mexico. We picked July 4th since I wouldn't have to use much of my vacation time, and it gave me months to prepare. They sent me more papers to sign, literature to read, and suggested podcasts to listen to in preparation. They recommended listening to the Shawn Ryan podcast, in which he articulately and clearly described his experience in Mexico with VETS.

Testimonials from those who had already completed the treatment reinforced the efficacy of these plants to help or even alleviate post trauma reactions. I started their pre-counseling sessions, which were sponsored and online. VETS had clearly thought through the pre and post treatment process. They would pay for the treatment and the follow up counseling sessions. They hired competent and credentialed therapists and facilitators. Many of their staff were veterans as well. I felt supported.

In time I began to feel optimistic about the possibility of "breaking through" the obstacles to my peace of mind and achieving a more productive life. The flat and dark feelings in my heart began to lift. I continued to pray for guidance.

In June 2022, the VETS organization sent me my ticket to San Diego along with instructions of where and when to meet the others for our ride down to Mexico.

At the appointed time and place I met the men who would be in our group for treatment. I think they were surprised an older woman like myself would be part of the group that was usually just Special Operations and Special Forces veterans. We piled in the car sent for us. They chatted on the way down to the border. I mostly listened.

Upon arrival we were introduced to the staff, shown our rooms and given a schedule. Their place was comfortable with tastefully placed artwork, books and a fully stocked kitchen. We began our first group meeting with introductions. There were veterans from each branch except the Coast Guard, and with varying degrees of deployment experience, although all of us had been to Iraq and some of us to both Afghanistan and Iraq.

We were each given physicals which included blood and urine tests and EKGs, followed by a review of our medical history and explanations of possible effects of the plant medicines we were about to ingest the next day. We were told to turn in our cell phones and any other electronics.

The food prepared for us was healthy and delicious. We were given time to journal and write down our intentions for this treatment. That night we had a fire on the grounds outside and, when we were ready, each of us threw our papers with our intentions into the fire. The smoke traveled up into the clear, star-filled sky. I felt the gravity of what we were about to undertake together.

The next morning, we ate a light breakfast and had a longer meeting with the chief facilitator, Jonathan. In addition, another Special Operations veteran joined us. He had gone through the plant medicine journey before and was there to provide guidance and support. He and the main facilitator told me they "heard about me" from Trevor who ran the majority of VETS programs. He happened to be on vacation the week we were there. I did wonder what was said about me, but didn't press them further.

We prepared for a sweat lodge as part of the ceremonial detoxification of body and spirit. The lodge was a short distance away by car. This was a differently constructed sweat lodge than I'd experienced with tribes in the USA and with Chief Archie Fire Lame Deer when he came to Australia. This was run by an elder Mexican woman and one of the women on staff. They spoke in Spanish and part of the chants may have been in another language. The younger woman translated.

When we were all seated and started sweating, the elder woman turned to me in semi-darkness and spoke. Her words were translated to the group.

She said, "This woman is full of light. I am honored she is here beside me." I bowed my head. I was embarrassed. She was speaking about me.

We continued the ceremony and gathered after to check-in with our facilitators. It was a ceremony that had similar aspects to Lakota inipis but also had very different protocols, language and construction.

I was taught, and I firmly believe, it is not my place to describe these ceremonies. They are meant to be sacred and experienced directly, not just read or written about. Others have already spoken about their experience in Mexico with VETS and other programs which incorporate sweat lodges.

I will say I felt cleansed, refreshed and relieved to be away from strictly medical examinations and procedures. We all showered in the outside showers before heading back to our base location.

We had individual talks with the facilitators and health professionals there, and staff continually monitored our vital signs. Before we received the first plant medicine-Ibogaine-we were given basic instructions, and each of us swallowed the first dose downstairs. Going up the stairs I felt the house was Escheresque. My body was already responding to the Ibogaine.

When we got to the upstairs room, we were each hooked up to monitors lined up along one side of the room. Each of us had a thin mattress and a black sleep mask to put on when we felt we needed to 'travel inward'. They put a large mirror in front of each of us.

Our mattresses were almost next to each other. Around us were health professionals and our facilitator. Music and drumming started as soon as all our monitors were checked. I was starting to 'trip'.

The music took me further into what was to be a dark ride. I felt I was being led into Dante's circles of hell...an Inferno.

One of the music selections was a song called *Kothbiro, by Ayub Ogada*. I recognized this song. I had given my son, Denali, the album. He told me he loved to paint to this music. How I loved to watch him paint. I felt tears welling up in my eyes. I saw many memories of my son, our family, my husband. They were alive in that room for a time and then they faded. The music kept changing and as it did, I was propelled into different parts of my past.

Nausea churned up inside me as I watched scenes from my life. I was powerless to stop it. Each of us had a small of bucket beside us we could vomit into. I purged. My whole body started trembling. I had to lie down. It felt like hundreds of electrical currents were coursing through me.

When I laid down, I felt partially excarnated from my body. I could see the others in the room. I could hear them. I could also see the scenes from my life. At one point, my right hand started moving as if I were back in the Joint Operations Center in Kabul, and I was clicking the mouse on a number of computers and those huge screens appeared in front of me. Myriad data was streaming across my sightline and Palantir-like links were forming on the 'screens'. The music sounded more in the distance.

I spiraled into another realm where I saw scenes from my work in Russia, in Pakistan, in Afghanistan, in Kurdistan, but I was on the outside of an event. This time I could see events happen from a 360 view. This was different from my usual memory of these events. My brain must have registered all this at the time, yet only focused on certain individuals, landscapes or actions in the moment. Now, I was seeing everything and everyone. Certain past traumatic events became clearer, but I was detached from the emotion. I continued to feel nauseous and vomited again.

I saw Marty, too. I saw him on a number of mountains. Then I saw him on K2 and I 'saw' what happened with him and our son, Denali. Marty was saying, "I didn't mean to kill him. I didn't mean to..."

I saw Denali briefly above me as if in a cloud. He was sorrowful. In my mind I wanted to call to him, but I couldn't. I felt nauseous again and had to relieve myself. A staff member must have sensed and came over to help me. I could hardly walk. He supported me to walk to the bathroom. He stood outside and waited till I finished and held me up to walk back to my place.

Others started vomiting or needing to go to the restroom. I lay back down, placed the sleep mask on and once again dove down into the next circle of the inferno of memories. This went on for hours and hours.

My mother had died a couple of weeks earlier, and scenes from my childhood flashed before me, but this time I saw them as an adult, without the powerlessness I had as a child. Other members of my family briefly appeared including those I loved dearly but who had died years before—my grandmothers, my grandfather, my aunts, uncles, friends, teachers, colleagues, teammates.

Just before dawn, I saw Marty again. He was in his USAF PJ uniform with his maroon beret. He was saluting me and then handing me a maroon beret. Instead of my US Army name tag, he showed me a USAF name tag that read 'Munisteri' and he said "Good job." I felt a sense of relief.

Then my body started trembling again and once more I went back to Siberia. The same disturbing event in Kemerovo was displayed in front of me as if I were viewing a movie; but I was in it, at the same time I was watching. We were all speaking Russian.

I lost all track of time. The music was still changing but the beats seemed slower and more melodic. I felt as if I were flying over the others in the room and could hear them. We were together in this etheric realm. I think I vomited one last time before I felt the medicine easing out of my body.

The journey lasted over twelve hours. Slowly I tried sitting up and taking off the eye covering. I was still weak. One of the staff came over and handed me tissues. She supported me to stand. Staff members took off the monitors on my chest and helped me walk downstairs and back to my private room. I think I asked for water before I passed out into a deep sleep.

That afternoon we all met again to share some of our experiences. VETS provided other modalities to help us integrate our encounters with the plant medicines. We had Reiki massages, yoga stretching class, and a Mexican woman energy healer who surveyed us individually and spoke to us after our first journey. We continued to be monitored by Western medicine means with daily vitals checks, intravenous drips, supplements or medicines as were indicated. I was offered aspirin (for my heart, I supposed). Every member of the staff spoke English and they all had a warm and compassionate manner. At least, this was my experience.

In the evening we had more meetings together and we watched a documentary about Ibogaine and about the Sonoran Desert toad, whose secretions created a potent medicine that we would be sampling next. During the film and after, the facilitator spoke about the need to conserve this species and therefore we were part of an experiment using 'synthesized' medicines. It was the first we were told of this. I was a bit disappointed.

To me the essence of a living animal would not be the same as just the chemicals created to replicate those of a living animal. However, the Sonoran toad population would probably be decimated once word circulated widely about the benefits of its secretion. Humans would upset the balance, and big pharma could capitalize on this new 'medicine'. I understood the reason for this decision.

The next day was in preparation for the 'Toad medicine' otherwise known as 5-MeO-DMT. Although people wrote and spoke about smoking it, in reality the facilitator or health practitioner created the smoke and blew it through a pipe or tube into your open mouth and nostrils. You inhaled it.

It was reported by hundreds of veterans treated, that this medicine made them feel "one with the universe, at peace," and that it was a soothing cap to the power of Ibogaine. One of our group declined. He felt he'd had enough to process with the Ibogaine. We were given the choice to say no to medicines or doses.

This time we were to go upstairs one by one and have the session individually. We were warned not to worry if we heard screams, shouts or all sorts of other noises. This would not be a long journey like Ibogaine. There were at least three staff there to support us.

When it was my turn, I entered the room, sat on the thin mattress and was told to relax. A staff member pointed out the pillow and said I would be falling back, and that he would be there to guide me to the pillow. He instructed me, "Close your eyes. Just let go, surrender to the medicine."

As he blew the smoke into my face, I felt I lost control of my body. I felt myself falling backwards. My eyes opened and I 'saw' my friend and teammate Lisa Akbari sitting right next to the staff member. I was still holding on to his hand, but now Lisa's hand was there. Lisa was in the clothes she was shot in, but there was no blood. She seemed peaceful.

"Don't go," I remember calling out to her. "Stay, please stay."

"You can let go now, Jo," she responded and started to fade.

Suddenly, I felt I was spiraling down into the circles of hell again.

I started speaking in a mixture of different languages. Arabic, Russian, Hebrew, French came flooding into my brain along with images of people. The words spilled out of my mouth. Traumatic events replayed before my eyes.

Then my back felt as if it were burning. I wanted to cool off and I think I kept saying, "Water, bottle of water." One of the staff handed me a bottle of water and a small towel. I remember putting it on my back to cool off.

Then a memory of terrible and violent situations played back in my mind but this time I could say, "Kaf ah!" Stop in Arabic.

More hellish memories came at me in a kaleidoscope of images. I felt short of breath. I was sweating profusely or so I thought. I wondered when the happy, peaceful feelings would start.

Slowly the room and the staff in the room came into view. I was lifted to sit up and given some water to drink. My 'ride' was over.

But I didn't feel at peace. I still felt the pain and more traumatic events replayed for a few minutes. I was shaking. I felt adrenaline seeping back into my system. Two staff members helped me to my feet and walked me to my room. Again, I collapsed into sleep. It was not the trip I expected.

Maybe I was a divergent. I told myself it didn't matter. I slept until dinnertime.

We spoke with each other, shared parts of our experience with the medicine, and shared a meal. The next day would be our last as a group. We were to debrief again in the morning.

One of the men who took the medicine after I did wanted to talk. We went out onto the grass and discussed our experiences. He didn't have the 'wonderful feeling of oneness' either. At least I didn't feel I was the odd one out after our conversation.

The next morning, we ate breakfast together, spoke more about our experiences, and prepared to leave in the afternoon for San Diego. The facilitator and staff returned our phones and other electronics. We were told about the follow up 'integration groups' it was recommended we join. Our vitals were taken once more and noted. Someone told me, "You look twenty years younger. You are glowing."

I looked carefully into each of our group members' faces. All our faces had changed at least slightly over the past few days. It was noticeable. We all looked lighter somehow.

We hugged all around and bid farewell to our Mexican staff. It was time to return to the USA. We drove in the summer sunlight back to the border checkpoint. I sat in the front and smiled at the border guards. They checked our passports then waved us through. I breathed a sigh of relief when we were let off at the airport. I was still buzzing when I boarded the plane for Texas.

The energy and buzz from my plant medicines lasted for months. I re-oriented myself over the last weeks of work in August, with my international team. Whenever I hopped on the computer for Zoom meetings, some of the electricity from the 'medicines' returned. It was distracting. I was also crying more when alone.

My need to process what I had been through in Mexico pushed me to read more about psychedelics, listen to the Shawn Ryan podcast again, and to Amber and Marcus Capone on the Jocko Willink podcast. I compared other veterans' experiences with mine. There were similarities.

I didn't have as much in common with the others in my all-women integration group, which met over Zoom. They were, for the most part, strong women who had to deal with their husbands who were in Special Operations. A few had been in different branches in the military, but none had been on the ground in conflict zones—at least not in the group meetings I attended.

The conversations were facilitated and directed. Only certain topics were selected and discussed. There were too many women to have any in-depth conversations in less than an hour. It was more frustrating than productive to take time away from work to do these meetings. I needed another way to re-integrate. I decided to have acupuncture to ground me.

My expert TCM doctor in Texas, had time for me. His treatment calmed my nervous system and he once again encouraged me to keep writing. Dr. Shen had treated both my children and me over the years. He was familiar with the challenges in our family.

VETS suggested private Zoom sessions to learn different breathing and meditation techniques. This facilitator was skilled. He had been with many veterans during their integration. After a short time, I felt a difference in my energy, my response to stress and a lessening of anxiety. I felt supported as I continued their on-screen breath sessions for the next year. And perhaps, for years to come.

In the summer of 2023, VETS suggested another group for integration. This was through Ambio, another contracting company for the program. This group consisted of both veterans and civilians who had taken the medicines. Again, the facilitators were skilled, but the session was only once a week for about 50 minutes allotted for everyone to speak and sometimes there were more than ten at a time on the session. Zoom does not grant privacy or information rights. They have the right to harvest all data and edit or sell the content from their platform. Zoom is partially owned by the Chinese Communist Party (CCP). This still concerns me and I hope they will find another platform.

Meanwhile, I decided once again to try and reconnect with my daughter Part of what I 'saw' during the medicine journey in Mexico was how much pain Sequoia was in. Her heart, soul and psychic pain became visible to me.

And I foresaw more pain for her. I hoped she would let me back into her and John's lives. I wanted to help and support them. I would try a different approach. I prayed for reconciliation.

Photo of Sonoran Desert Toad

Tabernanthe Iboga or "Iboga" plant in Central Africa

# CHAPTER THREE

# Moose & Mukluks

At the turn of the new year 2020, I was living and working in Kurdistan, Iraq. It was a chilly winter and people everywhere were coughing and sneezing. I didn't take much notice. We were in close quarters, huddled together in a van and transported to work in the early morning then brought back to our apartments in the late afternoon. Taxi drivers were coughing and commenting on the harshness of the cold winds. Children were coming down with fevers, and there were rumors of a strange, lingering flu from China.

My work this time in Kurdistan was with an international school. I was hired as a teacher mentor and also co-taught with teachers in the elementary sector. There were Kurdish, Assyrian, Armenian and Syrian families enrolled. But the school's principal, we found out, was a convicted fraudster, an Albanian American who had scammed school districts in the USA. He was an alcoholic and much worse, a predator. He pressured young, attractive teachers to perform sexual favors to keep their jobs. He pimped them out to his connections in Erbil, the capital of Kurdistan. He preyed upon the vulnerable.

Worse, it was suspected he 'traded' children he had supervision over in the refugee programs. Some young children were taken from school for a few hours during the day and then returned. We doubted their parents knew. A few of us compiled evidence before going to the US embassy in Erbil to report him. Unfortunately, as I had experienced before in my career, the US embassy said they could do nothing since this was Iraq. We decided to try another route to exposing him, but it would take time.

By February, 2020, there were reports of hundreds of Iranians across the border dying from this new illness. My colleagues and I all got sick with varying symptoms of this flu. We all recovered. Children around us in the refugee camps and schools also came down with this flu. They also recovered.

At the end of February, the governments of Iraq and Iran made the decision to prohibit flights from China. There was tension in the air in Erbil, where I lived. It was rumored the airport in Erbil was going to close again. It had been closed in 2018 into 2019, by the Iraq government to all but domestic flights. All expats would have to leave if we didn't have an Iraqi visa. Living in Kurdistan, this wasn't necessary, although I had obtained one for my previous work in Iraq in 2017-2018, with the Catholic University in Erbil.

Then, March 2nd, it was announced the airport would close to international flights. Quickly, we booked flights out through Turkey and left the next day. No one wanted to be caught in a major health emergency in northern Iraq.

In March of 2020, much of the world changed. Leadership in most countries were in panic mode. There seemed to be an illness which spread quickly, as a virus would, confusing medical and public health experts and causing grave concern. They said this was a new virus

Author in front of Mar Elia church in Ankawa, Iraq – March 2020

they hadn't seen before. They were predicting that millions would die from this flu unless severe measures were taken. They decided to mandate new protocols for entire populations. Not just the ones who were symptomatically ill, but for all people in their jurisdictions. They stated these restrictions would be for the general good as "we are all in this together".

Quarantine, a word not used for many decades, became a term in common use. People were required to be restricted to their homes or, if traveling, to hotel rooms for weeks at a time before being permitted to move among the general population. Makeshift testing stations popped up in transport stations, health clinics, pharmacies, school buildings, airports and grocery stores.

Mask mandates required all people in certain areas both outside and inside, to wear a face covering. There were no real standards that made any sense in terms of materials used, the way they were worn or how sanitary the face coverings were. In general, your mouth and nose needed to be covered although you could remove the covering to eat and drink in a public space. It made no scientific, logical or medical sense, but people dutifully complied out of ignorance and fear.

As I transited through Istanbul, Washington, D.C., and Austin, more and more mandates were imposed. I sent an email asking if a job in curriculum and teacher mentorship in remote Alaska was still open. I received an affirmative response and a contract to sign. The stipulation was I had to arrive in Alaska by the end of March 2020, before everything closed down and it might not be possible to get into the Yupik communities.

I arrived the day after my birthday in March 2020, to the small, crowded airport in Bethel, Alaska. It was snowing, freezing and grey, but I was happy to be in my new place of employment. It was my first visit to Alaska after years of hearing about it from my husband. I had a few hours' layover in Anchorage, and it was daylight. I could see portions of the Alaskan mountain range covered in snow out of the large airport windows. The view was stunning.

This was Marty's favorite post when he was serving in the US Air Force PJs (Special Operations Pararescue). This was also the mountain range that included Denali, the mountain our son was named after. The Alaskan range was where he and his father created a new route in 2011, that they named 'Dad and Son' two years before their death on the mountain K2, in Pakistan.

I felt privileged to be in Alaska and in Bethel, a place where more than 90% of the population were Indigenous Yupik. These were some of the hardiest people on the planet, from what I had heard.

Fortunately, all my luggage arrived safely. People were already wearing masks on their faces. I searched for my boss, who had sent me her photo. She told me she would be picking me up and taking me right over to tribal housing where I would have to be quarantined for the next two weeks.

We found each other. She looked me up and down, checking my boots and outerwear, and gave me a nod, satisfied I was prepared for the weather outside.

"Hi, welcome. Is that everything you have?" She asked.

"Yes, it's all here. Thank you for picking me up. My phone doesn't seem to work up here to call a taxi."

"No, it won't." She laughed. "We have a different provider for cell phones and the internet...when it works. I can get a sim card for you so you'll be able to text and check email until we get an internet line into the apartment. Meantime, I'll be able to go shopping for you and come by since neither of us are sick. But you can't go to the admin building where we work for at least two weeks. Sorry."

"Ok, I'm glad at least we can see each other and you already know the ropes."

"Oh, yeah. I've been here for about fifteen years already. There's not much here in Bethel. You'll find everything soon enough. It's not that big."

We packed my suitcases in her station wagon and drove to a set of rundown apartment units that were part of the Yupik tribal housing. Every building was on stilts since the snows could pile up to six feet high or more.

We carried my bags up the slippery wooden steps. My boss had metal 'moose tracks' attached to her boots which gripped the surface and prevented slips and falls. I remember hearing about them when I was in Siberia in 2011-2012, but no one had them in Novosibirsk. At least from what I saw being there in the winter. I made a mental note to buy some. I also wanted to try the Yupik footwear made of hides called mukluks.

The apartment was sweltering hot. I was stunned. This was not what I expected.

"The thermostat is broken. Someone turned it up to 80 degrees, believe it or not, and they won't be able to get someone to fix it until you finish your two-week quarantine. We can open the windows to cool it down and get some fresh air."

The apartment had two floors, two bedrooms and two bathrooms. It was meant for a family, but I was grateful for the space. It was sparsely furnished with everything I needed including all appliances except for a washer and dryer. To do your laundry you needed to go outside and over to the next building. You had to bundle up to wash and dry your clothes. It was a coin operated facility.

My boss explained the rules to me.

"Technically this is a dry town. No alcohol but you'll see that's not really enforced. All utilities except the internet are included so don't worry about paying for this extra heat. If you break anything or anything is already broken let me know so they don't charge you when you move out. The elementary school, grocery store and main administration building for the school district are all within walking distance. I live down the street near the walkway which is covered in snow right now, but a great place to go for walks when the weather lifts."

"I'll bring you your Mac computer. We are sponsored by Apple. They provide our work computers and laptops. It looks like much of our work will be online for the next few months with the outlying villages. Tomorrow, we have a Zoom call with the rest of our team of instruction coaches. The electricity goes off sometimes and the internet is unreliable, just so you know."

"Actually, I'm used to that in the places I've worked overseas. I'm adaptable." I reassured her.

"Oh, and we are not called mentors anymore, we're called coaches, but the job description hasn't changed. Each instructional coach chooses five or six schools and villages for the next school year to mentor. The remainder of this school year will probably not resume in-person teaching, from what I hear from the board."

I was disappointed to hear this, but hoped that wouldn't be the case after the summer.

I yearned to go outside and explore more of my surroundings while it was still light. In March, the days were still short and the nights long in Alaska.

"See you later. Thanks again!"

I waved to my boss as she exited down the stairs. She was an attractive woman, half Chinese from her mother's side and half Irish-American from her father. She had a jaunty demeanor from what I could tell on first meeting. She would be my immediate supervisor for the next two contracts I did with the Lower Kuskokwim School District (LKSD).

"Oh, Joanne, wait." She warned. "Don't drink the tap water. I left you bottled water and some food in the fridge. The water here is very hard and not drinkable."

When I shut the door and opened the windows, I relaxed. It was around lunchtime. I needed to get used to the time.

I always packed a small battery-operated alarm clock. I set it to the local time, then took off my watch, an accessory I didn't like to wear except when traveling.

In the refrigerator were two cases of bottled water, white bread, cereal, cans of soup, some cinnamon buns, instant coffee and a carton of milk. I sighed. Luckily, I brought my own tea, cans of tuna, some spices and beef jerky. I wouldn't starve.

I reflected on the fact that I had just come halfway across the world from Iraq, a country ravaged by war for decades, and considered a third world country, where you couldn't drink the water and electricity was unreliable, to the far north of the United States in 2020, where you also couldn't drink the water and electricity is unreliable.

While I was unpacking in the bedroom, I heard noises from next door through the wall. Children playing, running up and down the stairs. This cheered me. There would be people around.

I made myself some tea and surveyed the area from my open window. The tribal housing was in a U-shape with two long buildings in each section. They were two stories, made of hardiplank. They all looked the same. Cars were parked in the middle and some attempt had been made at plowing, but snow was piled high, and a thick layer of ice showed underneath. It would be treacherous walking on the ice. I remembered the experience from my time in Novosibirsk, Siberia, in the winter of 2011-2012. The difference here were the constant winds. I read they often gusted up to 25 miles per hour off the river, robust enough to literally blow me over.

My boots had some traction, so I ventured out. The air was calm and cold. I made my way down the stairs and walked about the units. There was evidence of children playing; some had left their bikes and toys outside. As I rounded the corner to find the grocery store a couple walked toward me. They looked Yupik to me, but I was still ignorant about the Yupik and Cupik people. There wasn't much available to read about them and it was better I learned in person from these people themselves. They glanced at me and nodded. I found out soon enough I was the only non-tribal person living in this housing.

There was not much on the snow-covered tundra except some houses, one grocery store and across the way, school administration buildings, an elementary school, a Russian Orthodox church, a gym and a small strip of stores. The church and gym were closed due to the mandates. The population of Bethel was listed as 6,000 although contract workers were not counted.

During the next week I met my neighbors on both sides.

There was a family of at least six people living on one side and another family of five on the other. Each family had children and the larger had a grandmother living with them. I saw the grandmother putting out a bag of trash on their landing. We met and she invited me in for coffee and asked me how I came to live there. Perhaps that was a polite way of asking how I came to live in tribal housing when I was evidently an outsider. Fair question. She was curious when I said I would be working with the Lower Kuskokwim School District and they had placed me here for my first contract. I offered to take down the trash bags since it was icy and I was going down that way. She nodded and

Taking a selfie near the St. Sophia Orthodox church in Bethel, Alaska

told me to just knock if I needed anything. Her grandchildren were shy and kept behind her as she let me out her door.

For two weeks, when I wasn't on Zoom meetings, or reading up on all their curriculum, I walked outside as much as possible in the daylight hours. After my quarantine was over, I walked to the LKSD administration building and back every day. It was only about a 15-minute walk and the bracing winds woke me up better than coffee.

Most people walking by didn't wear masks except when they had to enter a store. If you didn't walk, taxis were the way to get around. Going anywhere in Bethel cost you

$5.00, and it was $8.00 to get to the airport. Most people in Bethel and other Yupik communities did not have their own vehicle. They would use snowmobiles or "snow gos" for most of the year and people shared rides and cars as well. There was a school bus provided for children to go to school, but schools were closed. We were told probably in the school year 2020-21 they would open.

LKSD is said to be Alaska's largest rural school district counting by the number of schools, students and staff. The district encompassed the lower part of the Kuskokwim River Delta, along the coast of the Bering Sea, located approximately 400 air miles west of Anchorage. They had 275 teachers and more than 100 staff over outlying villages and islands.

Each instructional coach was responsible for 5-6 schools. This included all teachers, principals, assistant principals and teaching assistant staff. Under normal circumstances we would travel to all our schools. Most required travel by small plane, but Raven Air Lines was also closed shortly after I arrived.

I was introduced to my other team members, the superintendent and her assistants, personnel, the tech department, the Army ROTC unit in the building, and the NEA union representatives. The union reps started pressing me right away to join.

I was shocked that none of the positions of real authority were people from the Yupik community. I found out no

Yupik members were principals of the schools in the villages and very few teachers were from the Yupik communities. The LKSD superintendent didn't even speak Yupik in what was advertised as a "bilingual district." She was from Idaho. Most other administrators and teachers were from California, Oregon, Washington, a few from other states. Most came here for the promise of a higher salary, but since the cost of living was so expensive, most did not end up saving as much as they believed they would. There was also a very high turnover rate for teachers.

To become certified under the present system, prospective teachers had to relocate to Anchorage or another major city in Alaska to do their undergraduate teaching degree and become state certified.

The majority of Yupik and Cupik from villages did not want to leave for three to four years. Theirs was a different culture from the cities and from other Alaskan tribes such as the larger

One of my colleagues, an administrative assistant, displaying her beadwork in the Yupik tradition. Inside the LKSD admin bldg. 2020.

Athabaskan nation. It would have been much more productive to train Yupik and Cupik teachers in their own communities.

While "Elders" would sometimes be invited to teach Indigenous crafts to students, or participate in festivals and storytelling, this was a minor part of the LKSD curriculum.

The more I read over the newer public-school curriculum for elementary and middle school students, the more aghast I became at what had become of the United States public school system or really, the public indoctrination system. I hadn't had contact with the USA public school system since 2005. A lot had changed for the worse in 15 years.

The 'Social, Emotional, Learning' (SEL) component of health subjects emphasized sexual content and was certainly inappropriate at best for young children, and definitely contrary to their tribal traditions for female and male roles and responsibilities for thousands of years. Sexual content even in kindergarten through fifth grade, was pornographic. Young children do not need, nor should they be taught in school about all sorts of sexual positions, lifestyles, 'identifications,' or about birth control.

The 'climate change' agenda was interwoven in every subject content. Children were/are being taught that "humans are the problem". They are supposed to be the hope of the next generations and encouraged.

The Yupik who worked in the administration building were either assistants to other higher admin positions, or part of the translation unit. A project, generously funded by the federal and state government, promoted translating all the curriculum into the Yupik language. However, the vast majority of teachers, even those who had been in LKSD for over ten years, did not speak the language. Therefore, teaching was not immersive and Yupik language was placed as a subject in school, separate from other academic subjects.

Worse, all sorts of data were being gathered and compiled on all students and their families. But this was not explained to them. The parents were not asked for their permission. Leadership deliberately excluded them in the process. Teachers would conduct surveys of their students about their home life without sharing the questions with parents or informing them of what the data would be used for. Questions were asked about firearms in their home, how many books were in their home and other topics that were none of the school district's business. Besides, children are not a reliable source of such information in most cases.

Over time I saw leadership based on fear and inexperience, as well as willful ignorance. There were many slurs and denigrating comments made in meetings where no Yupik were present. Comments were made constantly about the "poor parenting," drugs and alcohol in families, "toxic masculinity in their culture," domestic abuse as part of their traditions, and other excuses for why learning reports and standardized testing scores were so low. Leaders in the district obviously had low expectations of their schools and students.

The low scores were also used to gain more grants and funding. Mental health issues were spotlighted for more staff (from outside the Yupik communities) and more medications. I had seen this strategy used a number of times in my career in education, both overseas and in the USA.

LKSD, I was to learn, was mired in scandals. Some of these scandals made it into state media. Sexual abuse from teachers and principals happened over years, with few investigations or prosecutions. This was a troubled district.

An undercurrent of fear ran through the Yupik communities ever since the great loss they suffered during the Spanish flu epidemic in the 1920s. Starting in 1918, thousands of Alaskan natives of all ages died from a sickness that was thought to be brought in by steamship passengers. Whole villages were decimated. There was a great loss of language, culture and confidence in traditional ways after that epidemic. It was slowly restored over the next fifty years, but then with the advent of new technologies, the discovery of lucrative natural resources in Alaska, and the introduction of hard drugs, the breakdown of culture, traditions and families accelerated.

It was a similar history to other Indigenous populations I had lived and worked with over the course of my life. From my analysis and experience, the breakdown was deliberately engineered. First, separate children from their parents, forbid their language to be spoken, take their lands and resources and demean their traditions and rites as "backward," "savage" or "superstitious." Then, bring in alcohol, drugs, processed foods, and their health and family unity will start to fall apart.

Fly in doctors and teachers who are on contract and don't live in the communities. Push medication and untested medical experiments and procedures, keep people dependent on these, and use tribal monies to continuously support these and no other means of health care.

In 2020, another tool was used to permeate family and tribal life in rural and remote Alaska. This tool gathered data for use by corporations and government agencies. It was offered "for free". This was a computer and internet connection. All children were loaned tablets/iPad and Chromebooks for their schoolwork. Apple Inc., the largest tech company in the world, had long ago realized lucrative opportunities by securing contracts with public school districts. They had a whole generation of consumers hooked on their products. The internet connection was upgraded in Bethel, although infrastructure for basic necessities such as indoor running water was not.

In 2020, water still had to be delivered and stored in most housing in Bethel, USA. In the outlying villages, there was no central sewage or sanitation system. People still used buckets and buried their human waste outside. The bucket was euphemistically called the "honey bucket".

Yet, now they had the internet and computers. The laptops and tablets had inset cameras which could be turned on remotely. Recording intimate family discussions and activities was now possible. Profiling families, their challenges, weaknesses, appetites, attitudes and even political views about local and national issues could be done without their consent or knowledge.

The "pandemic" was a fiat for thrusting the Yupik, Cupik, and other Indigenous communities into the vortex of surveillance and psychological operations.

At work we were subjected to hours per week of new professional development courses which were required. We had more databases to learn, "Diversity, Equity and Inclusion" (DEI) rules to digest, and training on new devices and programs. Some of the district-wide meetings on screens with Zoom or Google Meet reminded me of the former Soviet, communist meetings described to me by my Russian colleagues.

Meetings would begin with a litany of "identities" spoken in almost reverent tones: "Good morning. My name is _____. My pronouns are _____. I identify as a _____. I acknowledge my _____ race/ancestry and able-bodied privilege." This was a sort of political confession for those who wanted to virtue signal. I shall cite an example:

New mandates were imposed by "health authorities" which made no health sense at all. For example, we had to make sure our desks and bodies were at least six feet apart from other human beings. We were directed to move our desks farther apart or be in separate rooms. We were isolated for the most part. Yet we were all inside with the same air circulating.

We had to wear masks in the corridors or public spaces except if we were drinking and/or eating. Then we could pull off our mask and replace it after drinking or eating. Many staff just kept a water bottle by their side and their mask off. You were permitted to have your mask off in the restroom but needed to refit it after leaving the restroom.

Some of the least occupied staff delighted in becoming "mask patrol" and reported on others who didn't have their masks on properly or were seen coming out of an office without their mask on. I was "reported" for coming out of the restroom and not putting my mask on fast enough. The atmosphere in the administration building was tense.

Outside was another world, thank God. I made it a point to walk to and from everywhere I could no matter what the weather. While the grim grey skies continued throughout the Spring, I noticed all sorts of life begin to bloom again on the tundra. More children were playing outside and started to recognize me. They showed me their snow people, or precious pieces of blue ice they found. They pulled each other on sleds and slid down the hills. Outside, we were free to be without masks. I took this photo of one of the boys in my neighborhood.

As the snows melted and the doughy, brown mud seeped in on the unpaved roads, I could hike over the walkways and view the different species of birds around Bethel. The

Yupik made soup out of fowl including swan and petrel soup, and ate grouse, ptarmigan and geese that flew in from Canada or Russia. Bird eggs are a delicacy. Ducks start returning to the larger puddles and ponds forming on the expanse of the tundra. The spring grasses can be boiled or fried with eggs.

Fishing is an integral part of surviving for the hunter-gatherer people of this part of Alaska. Fortunately, a few of my colleagues invited me to come along and try smelting as soon as the river broke up. This was an exciting event each year, a celebration of nature, with the large ice floes moaning and whistling as they were carried downstream. It meant the rivers could be navigated again, and the fish could be caught.

Smelting is done with a net, not a line. The river currents can be strong. You need to place your feet firmly and be willing to be patient. My first time out I caught heaps of herring. I took them home, cleaned them and made herring soup and had herring with eggs for breakfast. A fine, salty start to my days.

In the summer more fishing is done with the variety of salmon being the prize catch, perfect for drying and storing for the winter. Families created their *fish camps* for generations. They pitched tents along the river and strung up lines to dry and smoke fish. They cut fresh fish into small chunks and made a "pickle" with them, storing them in jars. The families barbecued fresh salmon, rainbow trout, northern pike, Arctic grayling, and a species called Sheefish.

My colleague invited me to go with her brother on their boat to fish for salmon on the Lower Kuskokwin. They used a Garmin to locate fish underwater. It was the first time I saw this instrument used for locating creatures. It was peaceful on the river that day. Mosquitoes hardly bothered us, and we enjoyed the silence and focus of being together outdoors. Between the three of us we only caught one salmon, but he was a big one. We split the catch.

Ordinarily there is a lucrative tourist fishing and hunting industry in this part of Alaska in the summer and Autumn, but due to strict restrictions, these were all closed for 2020 and into 2021. The economies of Yupik and Cupik villages and towns endured even more hardships.

Author smelting on the Lower Kuskokwim River.
Spring 2020. Photo by Maria.

Before I went to Alaska, while I was working in Iraq, my daughter, Sequoia, had met a fine Irishman John McEvoy. They met while skydiving in California. They got engaged and my father urged them to get legally married since they were planning on buying property together in Idaho. My daughter mostly listened to her grandfather so they arranged a civil ceremony in my father's home city of Houston, Texas, in December of 2019.

John had been working in the USA for over five years. They both were serious BASE jumpers which made my heart beat too fast when they sent videos of their jumps and travels. They planned a lively wedding in Ireland for the next summer and asked me to help. I hadn't seen them except on screens for about a year. I was happy to oblige and found an actual castle in Cork, Ireland, which hosted weddings. We made the arrangements via email.

I invited them up to Alaska. I knew Sequoia and John would be interested in the Yupik and "Eskimo culture" as well as the mountains and connection to our family. But the mandates were in full effect in the summer of 2020. You had to be an 'essential worker' with an official letter to prove your reason for going to remote areas such as Bethel. We decided their trip could wait.

They had bought a house and invited me down to Idaho. I had a week of vacation, and Sequoia sent me listings for small houses near theirs and recommended I buy one. She said she had friends who could rent the property from me for the next year since I had already signed a contract through the 2021 school year. I looked carefully at the listings she sent and watched videos of three houses she thought I would like. They were near their home.

I made plans to fly down in June 2020, to see them and buy a house. It would be the first house I had bought in the US since moving back from New Zealand in 2006. I never thought I would buy a house in a state I had never lived in, but it was a chance to be near my daughter and her husband as they started their life together.

In the middle of May 2020, I was told I could no longer live in tribal housing. There was no warning. LKSD did this after I signed my next contract. Housing was very expensive in Bethel for non-tribal people. Utilities were also expensive.

A teacher who was leaving showed me her small place. It was essentially a container housing unit (CHU) similar to those on military bases, except it has a self-contained small kitchen and bathroom. It was down the street from the Saint Sophia Russian Orthodox church, and about a 20-minute walk to work. There were two CHU units to a block. The top level housed an US Army helicopter pilot who worked search and rescue. He had a different schedule than I did and he was friendly and helpful. I signed a lease and recalculated my budget for the next year.

Saint Sophia church in May, Bethel Alaska.
Photo by author.

My trip to Idaho went smoothly. I saw the house and building they purchased in Twin Falls. It was a town with its own beauty and character. It seemed quite safe. I found an excellent Traditional Chinese Medicine doctor which meant this was a place I could possibly live and have access to healthcare I knew and benefitted from.

I met John and Sequoia's young friends and showed them what I would need done on the house. I agreed to a low rent per month provided they did repairs and did some painting on my house.

My vacation week went by quickly. I watched them both BASE jump with their chutes off the famous Perrine bridge, played with their two puppies, and helped with their house and land chores. They were settling in well, but I sensed a dark cloud around my son-in-law. He was concerned about a fellow jumper who had gone missing. But it was more than that. However, I kept my feelings to myself and flew back to Bethel at the end of June 2020.

In July, the "midnight sun" was in full force. My CHU had thick curtains to block out the light, when necessary. I was deep in sleep one night in early July, when I woke to the sound of a loud thump near my bed. I had only one chair in the main room that doubled as my bedroom. The sound came from that chair. As I opened my eyes I saw my son, Denali, sitting there. He was more translucent and grayer than his living self. He had a serious countenance and looked straight at me.

I hardly had time to gasp, and wanted to run to him, when I heard him say, "Mum. Prepare."

That's all his spirit said before he dissolved into air. It was my son's first "visitation" while I was in Alaska. It was also the same month in which he had died in the mountains seven years before, in 2013.

I stayed in bed for a few minutes to see if Denali would return. I needed to sort through his short, but grave message. Deep down I knew something very difficult was about to happen. But to whom? What?

I decided to walk up to the Orthodox church. It was still closed, but it was a sanctified place of prayer. I felt I needed the "armor of God" for what I had just witnessed. My son had traveled between worlds to forewarn me.

For the next two days, in 24-hour sunlight, I walked about as much as I could. The mosquitoes swarmed. A cruel part of summer in Bethel.

Then, very early in the morning my time, my daughter called, distraught. Her husband had a stroke. John was only 35, an athlete in excellent health. It hit him suddenly while at work. They were at the hospital in Idaho. He was undergoing tests. They were trying to discern the cause.

As much as I could over the phone, I offered words of comfort. I offered to come down to help.

"Wait, Mum. We have to find out more about what happened. We might have to go to another hospital. When I know more, I'll let you know."

"Alright love. I do have to ask you, did you both get health insurance? Remember I mentioned this when I visited? This will cost quite a bit especially if he needs continuing care."

"No, Mum, but could you research any programs he could be part of? He's not a US citizen though. I'm looking online and talking to the hospital about possible resources."

"Good. I'll do some research and when you know more from the doctors call me, Sequoia. Anytime, day or night. You are both in my prayers. Love you."

"Love you too, Mum".

I lay back down, turned my head on my pillow to look at the chair where Denali had visited and warned me. I pondered what more I should prepare for.

Fortunately, John recovered from the stroke and tests indicated a hole in his heart they could repair with an operation in a Boise hospital. They also discovered a rare paraganglioma tumor at the base of his skull. They couldn't remove it right away, but would monitor it and pray it did not secrete more adrenaline and cause another stroke. This next one could be fatal. For now, God had granted us all a blessing and John's health was restored within a few months.

Some of my colleagues became friends over the year. They invited me to come butcher a moose they had been gifted. The local community often gave teachers and medical practitioners food they sourced rather than money. It was good to trade.

They taught me how to use an ulu, a semicircular blade knife the Yupik used to butcher. We sat in a group and butchered for one whole Saturday. We could each take home how much moose we needed. I was thrilled.

Joe and Maria butchering moose in Bethel, Alaska 2021. Photo by author

In my mind I had a new recipe to try using what ingredients were available in the sparsely stocked local grocery store and food I had ordered in by post. Coconut oil to braise the moose chunks. Canned tomatoes, cinnamon, onions, garlic, Bragg and natural apple cider vinegar with filtered water for the broth. I cooked it all in a crock pot for hours and shared the results with my Yupik and non-Yupik colleagues. They all approved my new recipe. I lived on moose

Handcrafted Ulu knife
used in Alaska

for months in 2021. I had a new favorite dish, moose stew. I had a new favorite knife, the ulu. I also had a full freezer for the rest of the school year.

The traditional practice of purification in steam baths and sweat lodges called 'Maqivik 'were banned as of March 2020. These practices promoted healthy and cleansed bodies, minds and spirits. Some continued anyway in family sweat lodges in the smaller villages. But the majority of those living in the Yupik and Cupik communities were influenced by scare tactics and feared reprisals. They submitted to the health authorities and stayed in their homes.

Meanwhile, deaths increased in my work area. The NEA teacher's union rep died in her sleep. She was only in her thirties but there was no official word on how and why she died.

As a local NEA union representative, she was reviewing my previous work for credit toward a higher salary. My case was put on hold instead of being transferred to another representative. I suspected so they could continue to pay me at a lesser rate.

The state NEA union rep sat near me and had continued to pressure me to join. It was her big club and I wasn't in it. Nor did I want to be. You had to pay a fee to join and they took a percentage of members' salaries. I didn't agree with most of their mission statement, or philosophy. I was content to do my job and avoid their politics.

Two young men who worked in maintenance died of 'Covid related' illnesses during the year. Treatment options were limited in the local clinics and hospitals. I had already stocked up on Ivermectin, Vitamins D, C and Zinc. Besides I'd already had and recovered from this enigmatic virus while in Iraq.

Like most in the area, I was excited about finally seeing the Spring Dance and cultural festival called Cama-i. But in 2021, the public health authorities and the public school district decided to ban the gathering and celebrations once again. This was a disappointing and unnecessary judgment. It negatively affected morale as well as the physical, emotional and spiritual health of the entire district.

In the summers of 2020 and 2021, most tours, popular vacation spots and national parks in Alaska were closed. Few park rangers were on duty.

In 2021, I planned my vacation days to hike and see more of the interior of this vast state. It would be my last chance

Author at Hatcher Pass, summer in Alaska.
Photo by friends.

to see this part of America, I reckoned. In some respects, finally seeing Denali National Park was a bit heart-rending for me. After decades of hearing about this part of Alaska naming our son after the mountain, going there made it clearer to me that *my Denali* was not there. And never would be again. Seeing the name Denali everywhere reminded me continually that my son was dead. This was not the reaction I anticipated. My friends in Alaska were very hospitable and tried to cheer me, but inside I was feeling forlorn.

My plans didn't include continuing with LKSD after 2021. Two contracts were enough for me. My spirit yearned for

more sun, more solace and more hope. The plane ride over the Alaskan range gave me a majestic view of this unique part of the USA, and our planet. I took a photo from my window seat and recalled the Yupik words "quyana tailuci" (thank you for coming).

The song "How Great Thou Art" played in my mind until we landed in Texas.

# CHAPTER FOUR

# TCM, Tunji and Master Li

The path to the Shaolin took me decades to find. I'd first heard of them while I lived on the border of Little Italy and Chinatown in New York City back in 1978-1985. Then again while I was working for the San Jose Repertory Theatre in California in 1986.

During rehearsals for Ken Jenkins new play, "007 Crossfire", I became friends with a cast member who was Chinese American. He took me to Chinatown in San Francisco and there introduced me to a Traditional Chinese Medicine healer who was skilled in acupuncture, martial arts and played the butterfly harp.

The front of his treatment center was an herbal pharmacy with dried plants hanging from the ceiling, a stone mortar and pedestal, pills, tinctures and boxes of needles displayed in shelves behind the front cases. Jade tools, glass jars with different colored powders, scrolls with Chinese writing and small green meditation chimes caught my eye as we bowed and said "ni hao" (hello) to this ancient looking man.

He looked at me for a few moments then nodded his head and indicated I should follow him back behind a screen to his clinic.

My colleague urged me to go and said he would wait for me. I walked slowly to another set of rooms which had sky blue walls and paintings of mountain scenes and flying birds. There were two massage tables with sheets and he pointed to one, then indicated I should sit down.

He sat in front of me and took my pulses on both wrists, looked at my tongue, and looked at the palms of my hand. He told me to take off my shoes and socks and lie down on my stomach. I placed my face in the round, donut hole at the end of the table and waited.

I'd had acupuncture before in New York City's Chinatown, but I was still nervous. Smells of herbs and incense filled the back room. The healer began inserting needles in my scalp, on the back of my neck, on the back of my legs, the sides of my ankles and soles of my feet.

Immediately I felt the electric rivers of Qi start to flow through the meridians in my body. There is no exact translation for Qi or Chi. The closest would be the Māori word "Wairua," which is loosely translated as "the energy or spirit that moves through everything."

I heard the healer step toward the side of the room and sit down on a raised platform. He took out an instrument with a long wooden bridge, strings, pegs and small soft hammers. It looked like a type of zither but I couldn't move my head to see more. Then he told me to "relax, breathe, listen."

Slowly he began to play this instrument. The music was similar to what I imagined tiny waterfalls would make. The sound was soothing and transported my mind to imaginary places far beyond the city of San Francisco and Chinatown. I felt I could swim on the air and the air was all different colors.

After about thirty minutes he stopped playing and came over to remove the needles. I felt released from any pain and calmly energized. He took my pulses again and looked into my eyes. He walked back to the front of his store as I put my socks and shoes on and hopped off the table.

The healer was speaking to my friend in Mandarin and taking down jars of herbs. He ground together several powders and plants and placed the mixture in a bag. He wrote a few instructions in English and handed it to me.

"You worry too much." The healer told me.

My friend grinned at me. It was true and he knew it.

"Xie xie," I said. Thank you. It was one of the few Mandarin words I knew at the time.

My friend told me that the Shaolin don't need to speak much. They communicate in silence. They are masters of the neutral. I didn't understand at the time what he meant.

My friend insisted on paying and we arranged to come back the following week.

As we exited, two matronly women turned their heads and stared at us. Here in Chinatown, I was definitely in the minority. The street signs and shop signs were in Mandarin and almost everyone walking about had Asian features. But I wasn't uncomfortable, just curious.

The next time I had direct contact with Chinese traditional medicine doctors and Shaolin trained martial artists was after we moved to New Zealand.

Before my daughter was born in Napier, I was introduced to a Chinese medical doctor and martial artist who practiced in Hawkes Bay. He was expert in qigong and many weapons, but his specialty was **Ja Shin Do.** He escaped to New Zealand from mainland China in the late 1980s, but his parents had to stay behind. There was a small but growing Chinese community in Hawkes Bay, but the greater numbers of Chinese at that time were in Auckland, Wellington and Christchurch.

This Traditional Chinese medicine doctor spent time while treating me with acupuncture, to explain some of the points he used and about the weapons he had displayed on his walls.

I was helping choreograph a new show for the Māori Performing Arts group Kahurangi. (For more background on my work with Kahurangi, see my book *Traveling Off the X*)

I decided to ask him if he would do a few workshops with my students and look at the possibility of incorporating some of the Ja Shin Do and Qigong movements into our dance sequences. He agreed to come meet the Takitumu trust elders and my boss, Tama Huata. He brought a few weapons with him: nun-chuks, Kwan Dao swords, a staff, a Shaolin saber, and a Snake spear. He was proficient with at least ten different weapons.

Tama Huata asked for a formal powhiri—an official Māori welcoming ceremony—for the newcomer. I called out with a karanga (a traditional Māori call done by women) I had been taught. In this way, he was escorted formally onto the grounds of the Performing Arts school. Tama asked him to introduce himself briefly and sing a song in his mother tongue of Mandarin. I had prepared him for this. He looked at me for a few seconds before he began his Eastern melody.

After we had greeted everyone with the Māori hongi (where you press foreheads and noses at the same time and breathe each other's breath) he stood in the center of the rehearsal hall and demonstrated some of his skills with his body and with the weapons he brought. Everyone paid close attention. When he finished, he bowed and Tama nodded to me.

Tama decided we would incorporate a section with the nunchucks, the Shaolin saber and staffs. The TCM doctor agreed, and we mapped out a schedule and times for rehearsal with the chosen cast members. They were to learn and incorporate martial arts moves within the larger performance. We co-conducted rehearsals.

This was my introduction to Shaolin moves, ways to warm up and train. It was grueling at times, but we were all keen to learn. One key was to be as relaxed as possible and be able to stop and start quickly. Shaolin moves are both fluid and dynamic. They change the energy around you and within you. The moves require control of all your limbs and tremendous abdominal and core strength to maintain positions with grace and balance.

Tama decided to call the new show "Taku Toa," roughly translated as "Our Strength." It's also a reference to the Māori proverb:

"Ehara taku toa i te toa takitahi, engari he toa takitini." Success is not the work of an individual, but the work of many.

This was a true collaboration of three cultures: Maori, American, Chinese.

After my daughter, Sequoia, was born on January 1, 1991, in Napier, New Zealand, this doctor helped me recover from a difficult birth. Sequoia accompanied me to many of my acupuncture appointments over the years and, along with her older brother, Denali, they were part of the Māori kohanga (meaning "language nest"). In this multi-generational, whanau-family-like school, I could do my work and have my children near me at all times.

This doctor also introduced me to the concept that the best Traditional Chinese Medical practitioners do not need to use herbs or even needles, *they can move chi around their body using their chi.* He showed me the first movements I learned of Qigong. They reminded me of some modern dance moves, but with a focus on the breath I had never been conscious of before. The forms were like slow duets when we practiced together. My internal alchemy started to shift.

Tunji with archery bow in China. Photo from his Facebook page.

It was many years later,that I formally studied Qigong as part of my training at the New Zealand School of Acupuncture and Traditional Chinese Medicine in Wellington, New Zealand. The founder of this institute was an American we called Tunji.

His full name was Adejola Musa Olatunji. His family was originally from the West Indies. Tunji first trained in acupuncture in Chicago, before studying martial arts and TCM in Taiwan and China in the 1970s.

He moved to New Zealand in the 1980s, then started treating patients in Wellington in 1987. In 1989, **Olatunji founded the New Zealand School of Acupuncture and TCM**. Not long after, he opened another branch in Auckland. As director, Tunji controlled the curriculum, taught, and treated patients in the two school clinics.

Tunji was a tall, strong and imposing presence in the school and he made it a point to know all his students. He seemed to make time for anyone who needed to speak to him.

Tunji made it compulsory for all students to take Qigong no matter what their specialty was—Herbal medicines, Acupuncture, Tuina.

Olatunji also insisted students get 100% on all their final exams in the first two years of classes in both TCM and Western medicine. He would ask us, "Do you want a doctor who didn't get 100% on their exams?"

Most tests would have bonus questions of up to 10 points or more, therefore it was possible to miss a couple of questions and still receive 100. But still, each year the first-year class lost a significant number of students who did not meet his standards.

The majority of his faculty were Chinese doctors who had fled from mainland China. Olatunji required us to learn the Mandarin names as well as the World Health Organization (WHO) numbers for acupuncture points. He taught us to be aware of the history and Chinese culture behind the names of the points and case studies.

Tunji had the gift of healing. As a black American, he stood out in Wellington, New Zealand, in the early 2000s. He was invited by local Māori to come to their maraes, and he encouraged Māori students to apply to his courses. By 2004, the school had extra clinics on weekends on different maraes led by a Māori graduate. I treated patients in these clinics in the North Island.

Tunji invited me to teach part time on his faculty after my first two years of study. He gave permission for a special clinic for Muslim women to be treated by only female TCM practitioners in the Wellington school building. We treated women from Iraq, Afghanistan, Sudan and Iran, who were refugees to New Zealand after 2003.

One of my teachers in Tuina—a special branch of Chinese medicine where the healer uses their hands for moving bones and medical massage—was originally from mainland China.

Olatunji in Wellington,
New Zealand.
Photo from Facebook

He had been an 'Iron Shirt' and trained with the Shaolin since he was nine years old.

The 'Iron Shirt' style of martial arts was for military use and cultivated power through Kung Fu and Qigong. After growing up with the Shaolin, he went on to become a medical doctor, and in New Zealand, he practiced both types of medicine, martial arts and Qigong. He was a hard task master. He used his English name of Steven. I secretly nicknamed him Shaolin Steve.

Shaolin Steve would only let you into his beginning Tuina class once you demonstrated you had trained your hand, thumbs and palms to be strong enough to grind down uncooked rice into a sand-like powder.

Each prospective student was given a pouch with two cups of uncooked rice, sewn shut at both ends like a pillow. You showed him your ground down pouch, but then he also had you work on his back with your thumbs, palms or fingers. His back was solid from his decades of training.

He told us a little about his training as a boy and one of the exercises they had to do was roll about with their shirts off in the winter, on wet gravel. His back was like a block of wood. If you did not have enough finger strength, he would brush you off like a fly and bark, "Practice more!" Or, as he told me once, "Not mature enough technique. More practice!" If Shaolin Steve let you work on his back for more than 10 seconds then you knew he found your technique acceptable or he would grunt in a form of approval. He was a man of few words.

Shaolin Steve demanded you know the Mandarin terms for Tuina techniques. He told us not to believe most of what was written about the Shaolin in "English books." He had brought out scrolls and books in Mandarin from China so they would not be destroyed by the Communist government.

It was evident Shifu (master) Steve revered and missed his Shaolin community in China, but it was impossible for him to live there anymore. He was frustrated he could not teach us as fully or as rigorously as he felt we needed, but New Zealand did not allow instructors to smack their students, or for us to study and work more than five days a week at the school. It was much different in China, as I was to find out later in my life.

In 2006, I had to leave New Zealand because of family disputes, and my children wanted to study and live in the USA again. I wasn't able to continue my martial arts and TCM practice while working to support them, but I continued reading about TCM medicine and the Shaolin.

One inspiring book I read was *Opening the Dragon Gate* by Chen Kaiguo and Zhen Shunchao (translated by Thomas

Cleary), an autobiographical account of a Taoist healer who escaped from China to San Francisco in the 20th century. I knew they had started a small training class in the Oakland area of California. On my computer I inserted a photo from a Shaolin performing group in China. It was in my mind to someday visit and study with them.

In 2010, Denali started his sophomore year at California College of the Arts in Oakland, California. I told him about the Shaolin and we decided to see if we could find out about them in Chinatown. He had already studied some qigong and meditation techniques in New Zealand. Denali was keen to continue in the USA.

Oakland has a larger Chinatown than San Francisco. We did find a qigong and Kung Fu training led by Shaolin monks in the back of a Chinese community center in Oakland. We were the only non-Asians visiting there, but I decided to ask permission to observe.

The Shifu looked at both of us and gestured with his hand for Denali to come over and train with the small class. I encouraged him to try. After the hour class, Denali was excited to learn more. We spoke briefly with the Shifu and explained that while Denali was busy most days with classes and work, he could come on Saturday mornings. The Shifu agreed for him to be part of the training. There was no set fee, they simply asked for donations and to be on time. Denali would have to ride his bicycle and carry it up to the training hall but that would be a good warm up. I watched him for his first week and then had to leave for my post in Pakistan. I was happy at least one of our family would train with the Shaolin.

Denali had learned meditation and some simple Qigong movements when he was in high school in New Zealand. One of the faculty, Peter Larking at the New Zealand School of Acupuncture and Traditional Chinese Medicine, agreed to take him on as a private student. Denali did his senior project for his final year at the Taikura Steiner School in Hastings, New Zealand, on his experience learning this discipline and applying it to doing more advanced skiing and back flips on snow.

Denali found an intersection with both forms of meditation and movement from the Japanese and Chinese cultures.

We discussed these crossovers, similarities and differences. Denali found the Shaolin training helped him with his studies, his concentration and his painting, but a few months into his study, he met a girl he wanted to pursue a serious relationship with. His priorities shifted. Denali decided because of time and focus, he needed to postpone his Shaolin training in Oakland.

We found a good TCM doctor near his university and Denali underwent a few treatments while he was attending, but he narrowed his physical training to skiing, biking, climbing and hiking. He thought, as we all did, that he would have plenty of time later in his life to return to meditation and martial arts. But that was not his destiny. He died on K2 in July 2013 at twenty-five years old.

After his untimely death, Sequoia and I compiled his writing and sketches into a book published with her company, Di Angelo Publications. We titled it as he had for his senior project: *Zen and the Art of Skiing* by Denali Schmidt. It was published in 2015.

Meanwhile, I continued to study Qigong when I could and found a new Shifu, Master Li Junfeng. He had been a prize-winning Wushu coach, director and actor in Chinese martial arts movies before being forced to leave China. He lived in the Philippines for a number of years and refined his forms. After developing his singular style of Shen Zheng Qigong, he moved to the USA. He was based in Texas but taught in different parts of the world including Europe and Israel. He accepted me as one of his students. He and his team made DVDs of his forms so we could continue to improve our techniques when we weren't able to participate in classes with Master Li in person. This was a useful tool for me since I was only able to return to Texas once a year with my contracting jobs.

Master Li decided to start a teacher certification training and testing in Israel. The course would last for two weeks. He was already in his seventies. I was given permission to leave Armenia, where I was teaching at the Yerevan State Medical University and helping to start a TCM introductory class and clinic, to complete my teacher certification of Shen Zhen Qigong and meditation with Master Li. Other teachers came from different parts of the world. We did this together on a kibbutz I had worked on as a young adult in my twenties, Kibbutz Sdot Yam. This kibbutz was right on the Mediterranean Sea with a thriving tourist business,

Master Li Junfeng
in Israel.
Author behind him. 2009

and in the summer of 2009, Israel was quite safe. There were few terrorist incidents.

It was refreshing to be by the sea and generate such strong qi together. I also reconnected with a TCM practitioner who had done a clinical rotation at Lincoln Hospital in the Bronx, New York, as I did. Naomi took me to her clinic and introduced me to other Israeli practitioners. TCM was integral to the Israeli national health care system, one of the best in the world.

In November 2012, I was the victim of a hit-and-run in Bastrop, Texas. My right shoulder and humerus bone were shattered. I had three fractured vertebrae, a broken collarbone, sprained ribs, a broken jaw and other injuries including a concussion. I was unconscious for quite some time.

At that point in my life, I was in the midst of training with the US Army to be part of their Human Terrain System (HTS) in Afghanistan. I needed operations on my jaw, replacements of my right shoulder and humerus bones, and surgery near my right eye. My goal was to recover in time to start the next HTS class intake in February 2013.

My TCM practitioners in Texas helped me through my recovery without the use of painkillers, but the after-surgery pain also thrust me into other realms of reality. In dreamlike, pain-filled days and weeks, I experienced excarnating from my body again. I also saw scenes from my future, although at the time I didn't know what they were. I had a glimpse of the psychic pain to come from loss.

The most powerful images I experienced were when I was unconscious and being airlifted to the hospital. I had a preview of the afterlife. I felt myself turning around swiftly and being pressed against a wall, like I was inside a centrifuge. Winds were blowing and whooshing past me and I saw a gray, tunnel-like place.

I started to walk down into the tunnel but was fearful of continuing when a wind blew me back. Then I heard and simultaneously saw a bright light and heard a whistling, rustling sound, and then I was suddenly back in my body and in the hospital.

I had the distinct feeling deep in my body and soul that "there is an afterlife" and that I had to be "better in the life I have left." For the first weeks after the operations, I felt "flat" and wasn't able to leave my body to leave the pain, as I had before. I kept remembering the tunnel scene and wanted to "go back" and explore, to leave the reality of this world.

But both my children still needed me. They were about to graduate from college. They were my incentive to push through the pain and recover enough to start another training class back at Fort Leavenworth, Kansas. I didn't want to worry them.

Looking back, I also had a preview of being with the Shaolin and being in the mountains in China, although at the time I didn't know that was where it was.[1]

In 2018, six years after being injured in a hit and run accident, I realized my right shoulder and arm were stiffening up. I was losing mobility while I was in Kurdistan, Iraq, this was concerning. I was told by the Orthopedic surgeon who had replaced my shoulder joint and right humerus with cobalt-chromium-molybdenum arthroplasty operation in 2012, that I would probably need another operation to cut through the scar tissue. This did not seem like the healthiest solution to me. I thanked him but decided to find other options.

---

1    See my book "Traveling Off the X" for more details about years 2012—2016

While I was waiting for a job teaching at what was supposed to be the new American University of Iraq in Baghdad, scheduled to open in late 2018; I decided to research the possibility of going to China.

Some of my TCM colleagues guided me. They warned against going to the CCP controlled area of Deng Feng for training, as it was very tourist focused. The more authentic and private training was not as advertised, and there were no tourists there. It was in Henan province, the birthplace of Kung Fu, up near a mountain called Yun Tai. I was given a contact email. A friend helped me translate my message into Mandarin as well.

Not long after sending it, I received an invitation. This enabled me to start the visa process. They would sponsor me for a year of training and a ten-year multiple entry visa.

Taking an entire year off for training in my sixties was a huge risk, but I strongly felt a "push" from beyond to take a chance now and not wait. As it turned out, the new university opening kept getting delayed due to political and security issues in Iraq. They pushed back the opening to September 2019. This was a sign to me that the time had come.

I returned to the States from Iraq to see my daughter and try to train while I waited on my visa. Sequoia was based in Los Angeles and Houston at that time. Her company was expanding. She was supportive of my venture and thought at one point she might join me there. She had visited China briefly as a teenager and in her early twenties.

When my visa came through, I left for winter training with a feeling of anticipation different from the feelings I had before when beginning a new position in a new country. This would be my first time to China other than transiting through Beijing enroute from Siberia, in 2012. I mentally prepared myself to be on the alert but also keep an open mind.

Years before, I had envisioned studying and training with the Shaolin. It was almost like an impossible dream that it could be realized in this lifetime. Now, that vision, dream, and plan were about to become my reality.

# CHAPTER FIVE

# The Shaolin

Yun Tai Shan International Martial Arts Training Center is a residential training center which only recently allowed a limited number of foreigners to train alongside their 600-700 children. The center has few modern conveniences and is located far away from any city. In 2018, few foreigners knew about this center.

They arranged for a driver to pick me up at the airport in Zhengzhou and make the two hour-plus drive at night to the center. He didn't speak any English but offered me a small, golden can of the Chinese version of Red Bull. It kept me awake and alert for the long ride. We arrived about 4:00 am to the front gates. It was November and already quite chilly.

The guard at the gate let us in, and a young man came running across the concrete courtyard. He took my large suitcase, and they explained in Mandarin that I was to follow him to my room.

All the female international students were housed on the sixth floor. There was no elevator, and the young shifu practically ran up the stairs ahead of me. I followed him to a room which he opened.

He turned on the light to show me my bed and the small bathroom. Then he showed me on his watch that I needed to be downstairs to eat at 7:00 am. I thanked him and looked at the simple room. The bed was a wooden platform with a foam mattress about two inches thick. There was one flat pillow, sheets, one towel and one face cloth. A metal bowl with chopsticks was on the windowsill. I assumed they were for me. There was no heat in the building.

Three plane flights, a long taxi ride and the time difference caught up with me. I collapsed on the bed. It was hard but I was thankful. I fell asleep almost immediately.

At what seemed like minutes later I heard commotion all around me. I looked at my phone. It was 5:30 am. I heard the sound of doors opening and closing, feet running on the cement corridors and stairs. It was still dark outside. I slid under the sheets and tried to go back to sleep.

At 6:00 I heard hundreds of children jogging in cadence to this Chinese phrase: "Ni hao Lao Tse, Ni hao Lao Tse."

I got up and looked out the window. In the dark hundreds were stretching, jogging around the courtyard and cement track. Shifus were watching, shouting and walking about observing their trainees.

I took a shower. Only cold water. I unpacked and changed into workout clothes before heading down the six flights to the courtyard. Seeing the only non-Asian faces in one group moving toward the stairs of another building, I decided to follow them. As I stepped onto the courtyard an elder man in a tracksuit approached me.

"Ni hao." Hello in Mandarin.

"Ni hao," I replied. I knew how to say, "My name is Joanne Munisteri" in Mandarin, and that I was from America (Mei gua).

He nodded and pointed to the international students group. I jogged over to them as they were entering a large building. On the first floor was a cafeteria and on the second floor a great training hall.

Some of the trainees scattered to different areas and started stretching again. One of the Shifus came over to me. He spoke some English.

"Welcome. You can watch now. Then we eat. Then we take you to the office to sign in and get your uniform. You start training after lunch."

"Yes, thank you, Shifu."

The Shifu shouted and three different groups formed quickly in three different sections of the training hall. They were for Sampa (full contact boxing), Kung Fu and Tai

Chi/Qigong. Each group had their own Shifu who started shouting directions for exercises everyone seemed to know. Push-ups, sit ups, sprints, kicks, spider crawls, jumps, squats. This went on for an hour.

Then each group stopped, bowed with the Kung Fu hand position to the center of their chest, then scrambled down the stairs to wait for breakfast.

There were about 30 international students. The majority were in the Kung Fu group. They ranged in age from teenage to thirties with the majority in their early twenties. Most were from Europe. Most were male.

One of the few female Kung Fu students came over to me and introduced herself. She was from France and spoke little English, so I switched to French. She guided me to the kitchen where I was given a small metal bowl, plain wooden chopsticks, and a metal spoon I could use. She introduced me to the head cook who was stirring soup in a huge cauldron pot with a long-handled metal spoon.

The international students were able to eat first. Shortly after we sat down with our soup, hundreds of Chinese children came in to have their meal.

We sat at long metal tables with fold down benches in the back while the children aged five to seventeen filled in by grade level with their teachers at their respective tables in front of us. Children were laughing, teasing each other and generally full of energy. Some openly stared at me, and

I heard a few say "pang de" (fat) and laugh. It was true—compared to the lean Shaolin, I was fat. Not by American standards, but by their standards, I would need to lose at least twenty pounds.

At the international student tables, most spoke German. A number of the trainees were from Austria, Germany and Switzerland. There were two from France, one from Spain and one originally from Algeria, but with a French passport. He spoke some English. The youngest was a girl from Russia who spoke English with an American accent and was conversant in Mandarin. This was her second year at Yun Tai, and she was fourteen. One of the girls from Switzerland was in the Tai Chi/Qigong group I was to train with. She was very helpful and filled me in on some of the rules.

You were given one bowl each meal, no more. If you wanted more food, there was a place across the courtyard where you could buy different food cooked to order. They only offered hot or cold water. If you wanted coffee or tea you had to buy it. You could only bring water into the training hall. No food.

Every infraction of the rules had a consequence, usually extra push-ups or extra clean up duties. You were never allowed to smoke, bring in or drink alcohol or illegal drugs. You were to ask permission to take a photo or video. No phones were allowed during training. Break any of those rules, and the punishment was immediate expulsion.

After eating, each of us went and washed our bowl and utensils at a communal trough-shaped sink and hurried outside or to our rooms. Females lived two to a room. Some males shared a room between three. I had my own room since I would also be teaching English for 2 hours a day to some of the Chinese teachers and younger children. I was also the eldest "trainee" at the center, and they still respected elders.

There were communal, open stall urinals and toilets on the first floor of the training hall/cafeteria building with no privacy. If you wanted privacy to relieve yourself, you had to go back to your room which meant crossing the courtyard and going up six flights of 24 stairs and down again. You needed to plan your eating, drinking and bathroom breaks carefully with the training schedule.

We were required to train in the uniform provided. If you wanted, you could buy another so you could rotate one to train in and one to wash. There were no dryers. We hung our uniforms on pipes inside or on the line outside,

depending on the weather.

There were two girls in Sampa, and the other four girls were in Kung Fu. They were all quite fit. I was not yet.

The young Shifu who helped me the night before was to be the Shifu I studied Qigong and Tai Chi with. He guided me to the office to get my student card, my track suit uniform, and my card to use for hot water. I was given an allowance for hot water the first week and thereafter I had to pay for time units of hot water.

I gathered all I was issued and went back upstairs to change for the next phase of training.

After breakfast, training resumed for three more hours. The Tai Chi forms were slow and fluid. My Shifu did not speak much but would come over and move a foot, hand, or parts of our body that were not in the exact position the form required.

Inside cover of my student card. Photo by author.

He also pushed us into stretches, sometimes sitting on our legs while we were in the splits position to help us attain the flexibility needed for high kicks. We repeated sequences of movements over and over until he decided we could learn the next section.

Concurrently, the other groups would be practicing fighting stances, weapons, boxing moves and acrobatics. The training floor was cement. We could pull out two-inch mats kept at the side of the hall if the Shifu instructed. Later I learned most training was done on concrete because your body and senses had to be alert and ready on any terrain. At times we did mountain running and slow forms out in a park area just outside the center.

Everyone started the morning at 6:00 am sharp. Arriving even one minute late would mean push-ups. Everyone trained outside for at least the first 20 minutes, no matter what the weather. We trained in rain, snow, high winds and sleet in the winter.

I saw the young children run out in the morning smiling, full of joy and energy. I rarely heard a child cough or come down with a cold the entire winter I was there: November 2018 to April 2019.

We didn't wear heavy coats in the cold. No gloves were allowed (10 push-ups for each hand in your pockets or in gloves). Only if a trainee had an earache or other condition could you wear earmuffs or a head covering. Training the head to be resilient, along with the rest of the body, is an aspect of Shaolin training often neglected in other martial arts and sports.

While we were at morning training, the children were doing academic studies. Everyone had a total of two hours for lunch and a rest. After lunch, their movement and martial arts training continued outside.

The international students trained for two or four hours depending on their level. If they trained for two hours physically then they had two hours of Chinese culture and language before supper.

High school grades practicing outside in the courtyard after lunch in December 2018. Yun Tai Center.

Everyone ate supper together. Usually, it was another bowl of soup or rice with vegetables, and once a week with chicken or fish. Soup broth was mostly made of cabbage which was grown outside the gates. The kitchen staff grew a number of vegetables, kept chickens and a few small dogs. Cabbage is a diuretic, so you had to be careful not to eat too much and then go train, especially if you wanted privacy and had to run up the stairs to your own room to relieve yourself.

One of the kitchen staff in front of cabbages harvested at Yun Tai International Training Center.
December 2018.

The children did not have snacks or any form of technology. No cellphones or iPad. There was no television anywhere. They played ping pong on outdoor tables, or basketball. They used chalk to make up games or draw on the cement outside. If the weather was clear, you could see many of the

7-to-12-year-olds practicing acrobatics and sparring outside on the grassy spots. There was lots of giggling, yelling and clapping with shouts of "Giayou!" as encouragement.

I was told this word "Giayou" referred to the oil that catches a spark to fuel a great fire. This was a reference to cooking in a wok-like pan where you heated oil, and then lit the oil for a quick blaze.

At any rate, we clapped and shouted "Giayou!" enthusiastically to encourage our fellow trainees.

Anytime I thought I was having a hard time doing the forms or exercises I would look over at the ten-year-olds

Children on break at Yun Tai International Martial Arts Training Center November 2018.

moving effortlessly through the movements and be both shamed and inspired to continue.

There were only a few girls in the high school classes and more in the elementary grades. I was told almost all the students were from families who had lineages with the Shaolin for generations.

A few of the boys still had a single braided que which they wore in the center falling straight down their back.

Although it was winter and quite cold in December, none of the main buildings had heating. The dorms had heaters on the wall but they were centrally controlled and did not go on until the evening no matter what the temperature during the day. We were initially permitted to turn on the heat for two hours at night from 9:00-11:00 pm after the last muster.

We were summoned to line up a number of times during the day and night. They translated the Mandarin word as "meetings" or "muster" in English. We would have to line up and stand in "neutral" with a neutral expression while they would observe us, check our uniforms, give us instructions, changes in schedule, announcements and sometimes "consequences" for not following rules.

There were individual consequences and group consequences. I will give you an example of an individual consequence from my first week training.

We had the possibility of using Wi-Fi for about two hours at night after training was done. I needed to get on the Wi-Fi one evening early in my time at Yun Tai, and one of the young women from Spain offered to help me. She did so after supper and let me stay in her room until the final meeting at 9:00 pm before the end of the day. The call to the final meeting was broadcast over the loudspeaker. I closed my laptop and ran downstairs to get in line.

The Shifu came over to us, looked up to the sixth floor and only one light was on. It was in the room where I had been using the Wi-Fi. My Spanish colleague gasped.

"Oh Dio. Oh No!"

Shifu asked whose room had the light on. She raised her hand.

"100 pushups. This is the second time for you."

I felt awful and raised my hand to explain.

"It was me, Shifu. I didn't know we had to turn off the lights. I'm sorry."

The Shifu looked hard at each of us. "Did you tell her the rules? She is new," he asked my Spanish friend.

"No, Shifu. I forgot."

"It is your responsibility to share this information. You do 100 pushups."

"Yes, Shifu" she responded and got down on the cold cement to start doing pushups.

"You," he said to me. "Now you know. All electricity must be turned off when you leave the room. Day and night. Next time, 50 pushups."

"Yes, Shifu." I responded. I could barely do ten pushups at that point. I wouldn't forget this rule.

Each Shifu counted his group members and dismissed us. My colleague continued doing push-ups. I felt terrible and hoped to make it up to her somehow.

I waited for her at the top of the 6th floor stairs. As she trudged up, she saw me.

"I love Kung Fu!" she said passionately. "It's true. Don't worry. It's not your fault. But really, I love Kung Fu!"

Only months later did I share this love and understand more of the Shaolin philosophy of collective responsibility at all times.

The first three weeks of training, I was in pain every day. A number of times I asked myself, inwardly, "Why am I doing this to myself?" But I knew I had to complete at least the first two months to gain any real understanding or benefit.

At least I didn't vomit as I heard many of the younger trainees did in their first days. Also, I wasn't the worst in every exercise. Shifu modified my exercises due to my right shoulder and arm injuries. I had to do push-ups on level surfaces, and going up stairs, but not down stairs.

Shifu asked me to give him permission to push my right shoulder against the wall and for him to circle my right arm around and back, since I couldn't do it fully myself. I almost felt the scar tissue tear again, but that's what was needed instead of surgery. I knew he was doing it to help me restore and rebuild my capacities to heal.

Early on, I noticed a pile of rocks stacked in one corner of the training hall. Soon I learned these were used in place of weights. Shifu asked each of us to choose a rock to train with. We used it for sit ups and carried it on mountain hikes. If you chose one, he considered too light, he replaced it. If you chose one he considered too heavy, he also replaced it.

One Shifu led mountain hiking each week and another Shifu pulled up the rear—which was usually me. I'd sprained my ankle in my second week, so I was slower than usual for a couple weeks while it healed. We were steered out of the center, past the village and into the hills.

At certain points both Kung Fu and Sampa students had to partner up and carry another student up and down a hill as part of the exercise. I didn't since the strain on my right shoulder and right ankle would have been too much for me.

I was able to have a few minutes to catch my breath and look over the evocative landscape.

Village outside of the Yun Tai Center main gate and before the mountain hiking trails. November 2018.

After the third week my body started to respond better to the training. We trained six days a week for a minimum of six hours a day. You could do an extra two hours at night, but that was optional.

However, we had 'exams' every two weeks in front of the other students and Shifus. Almost everyone needed the extra hours in the evening to practice forms for the tests.

The Shifus videotaped each of these exams. Afterwards, we would watch ourselves and they would point out mistakes. These video recordings were used as a tool.

Sampa students would fight every two weeks. They fought three rounds, and the Shifus picked each set of opponents. Females fought females and males fought males. I witnessed a number of injuries during the fights, but the Shifus would decide if they should continue or stop. Most times they let the fight continue no matter a black eye, bloody nose, or injured leg or ankle. The younger Sampa students could watch our exams, and we could watch theirs.

Walking about the campus, I would see some children with bruises over an eye or marks on their arms. This was a warrior culture. Fighting was normal. The youngest children of the Shaolin families living there would imitate the Shifus and teenagers fighting. They would hold up their little fists and shake them or try to go down into a horse stance (Mabou) and shout.

Children under the age of five were cherished and allowed to play on their own. There was a Chinese saying: "Until the age of five the child is master of the house. From five until twelve, the parents must be master, or afterward there will be trouble." Shaolin training ideally starts at five or six years old.

The first month the only contact I had directly with the Master Shifu was his stern corrections. He taught the Kung Fu group which trained parallel to us on the training mats, but he seemed to see everyone and hear quite well.

In December it started to snow. We were given a thin blanket and could buy warmers, sometimes called "Hot

Training hall in December 2018, with Yun Tai Middle school Sampa students waiting to fight.

Hands," little packets that produce heat when exposed to air, but they should not be put directly on the skin.

We were not allowed to wear gloves during the training day. We did warm up exercises outside with our hands exposed, and I was given a staff to start my weapons training. The exercises were similar to beginning exercises I learned in high school when I was a baton twirler. The staff was longer and made of wood but the action using my wrists and arms was the same. My right hand, arm and shoulder began to loosen and gain greater range of motion. I enjoyed practice with the staff, moving it in different directions.

Training exercises were almost always done in six directions—going forward, backward, right, left, up and down—and at two speeds, fast and slow. There were a number of basic warm up calisthenic-type movements, but the Shifus never did them in the same order every day. We couldn't predict what came next. This kept our bodies and minds alert and adaptable. You could not get by on autopilot. There were different numbers of repetitions depending on how your Shifu saw you were doing. Abdominal exercises, kicking, striking, extensions, horse stance, breathing exercises, head and neck rotations and strengthening, balance exercises, concentration, acrobatics and vocal exercises—the list goes on.

Learning how to push forth your voice together with movement and fully release while not straining is a skill. Most places I trained martial arts in the USA and New Zealand, did not incorporate the voice. They might say "louder" if you were counting or let you grunt in exertion, but the technique of using it as integral to fighting was not discussed.

At Yun Tai, sound was part of our training. Release sound from the diaphragm and you gain more energy. Like Shakespeare said of love in *Romeo and Juliet*: "My love is deep. It is as boundless as the sea. The more I give to thee, the more I have for both are infinite."

To me, it was the same with Qi. I had to adjust my mindset. I would always have enough energy or Qi if I knew how to circulate and generate it from within. Ultimately, it is boundless, like love. The literal translation for *Qi* is 'life force' and *gong* means 'work'. It hearkens back to a Hebrew saying "Life is work and work is life." It is all circular and spirals together. Human beings are all related. We have much in common.

\* \* \*

The Shifus decided they would host a Christmas performance presentation at the center. For the first time, family members would be invited. I was asked if I could teach some of the younger children to sing 'Jingle Bells' in English, and we (the international trainees) would be taught a song in Mandarin. We would use the nighttime extra practice hours to learn these pieces.

Usually, all ages wore the same track suit uniforms every day, but for this performance each class would have costumes. The entire center hummed with energy and anticipation for weeks.

Rehearsals for each class were directed with a serious attitude, no matter what the age of the performers. The day before the show, the courtyard was transformed. A stage was assembled, chairs were brought in for hundreds to watch, and a large screen was raised and permanently affixed to the outside of the main dormitory building facing the courtyard. This was a new requirement for the school. It would serve as a way for the Chinese Communist Party (CCP) to transmit and indoctrinate every week from the CCP broadcasting service.

The Chinese Communist Party (CCP) demanded every school broadcast the President and General Secretary of the CCP, Xi Jinping's message, every Monday to all students and staff on the big screens. All of us at Yun Tai were required to attend.

In addition, surveillance cameras were delivered and installed outside. The cameras could see our reactions to the broadcasts. They faced the courtyard. This was the beginning of the end of privacy for this secluded school and training center.

December 2018 Christmas show performance at Yun Tai. Five- and six-year-olds performing in costume outside.

A week before Christmas, the Shifus bought us decorations we could use to cheer up our corridors and rooms. We put tinsel on the handrails, set up an indoor Christmas tree and hung brown-eyed Santa faces on the walls. Between all of the international trainees—some from Germany, France, Austria, Spain, Norway, Switzerland, two of us from the USA, one from Russia, and one from Sri Lanka—we had lively discussions deciding what to put up where. We all cooperated.

We had heard the leader of the CCP had forbidden any Christian or 'foreign religion' expressions of celebration. People were being arrested in nearby cities for going to church or publicly displaying Christian or Christmas symbols. But away from any towns or surveillance, we were able to conduct our own festivals. We were able to rejoice in our own way.

Dorm decorations in our hall for Christmas 2018, at Yun Tai.

On Christmas day, the Shifus arranged for 22 of us to be driven with them into Jiaozuo. We all went to a restaurant, and were given free time to walk about and go shopping. They paid for the buffet meal and warned us only to portion out what we could finish.

Apparently, there was a law about wasting food in public venues. The customer and/or the venue could be fined if food was seen being thrown away. This reflected the difference in policy and culture compared to the West, particularly in America.

Upon return to Yun Tai Center, we were instructed to line up just inside the gates and place whatever packages or backpacks we had in front of us and open them. The Shifus started inspecting bags and stopped in front of one of the French trainees. This man was originally from Algeria and had been hassling most of the young women. The Master Shifu opened his backpack wide and pulled out two bottles of alcohol. This was strictly forbidden.

The man started to speak, but the Shifu put up his hand to stop him. The Shifu said in English, "Go upstairs. Pack all your things. You will be taken to the airport. You are no longer welcome here. You have broken our rules."

Two more Shifus came over and escorted him upstairs. One of the guards came forward and finished inspecting our bags. He nodded, dismissing us to our rooms. It was a sobering end to our night out. None of us were sorry to see this man leave.

Until December 2018, there were few outside visitors to Yun Tai or inspectors from any branch of the government. But that was to change in the next few months.

A week after Christmas a few new trainees from Germany arrived. Someone had created a Facebook page in German and French about training at the center. More people were starting to know about this training away from Deng Feng, and it was quite inexpensive by European and American standards.

As we were jogging outside in the early morning darkness, I noticed one of the new trainees who was very tall and thin. He was running, not jogging and the shifus cautioned him to slow down and pace himself. However, he was stubborn and disregarded the advice.

Once inside the training hall, the Shifus shouted out instructions and started the morning training with a brisk pace. The Master Shifu was on holiday with his wife and daughters. The younger Shifus took over.

This tall German man was doing sprints with us and was placed opposite me. As I was running toward the side wall, he ran toward me from the opposite wall. I noticed he was very pale and breathing heavily.

Suddenly, I saw him black out and his body begin to fall. Immediately I ran toward him to try and stop him from hitting the concrete. Everyone else around us was running away except our Shifu. He and I arrived just as the man fell and split his chin on the concrete. He was unconscious. I turned him on his side and looked around for a first aid kit. I asked the young Russian girl to translate and find out if there was a kit anywhere nearby. There wasn't.

I didn't have my acupuncture kit with me, and people were starting to panic. I knew a few points that would bring him to consciousness and used one of my hair pins and fingernails to press into his clammy skin. After a few more seconds his eyelids moved and he opened his eyes.

Shifu stopped his chin bleeding with his jacket. We lifted the man to a sitting position. He had a deep gash and it needed stitches.

After a few phone calls and translation to English by another German trainee, it was decided he needed to be taken to the hospital which was over an hour away by car. It surprised me there was no medical or first aid kits in the training hall or dining hall, but standards of care and hygiene are different in different countries. I decided to put one together for the training hall. I had extra supplies and could buy basic bandages in town that weekend.

The German man returned from the hospital in the afternoon. He had stitches on his chin and was given medication. He had a thyroid condition he had neglected to disclose on his application form. He would need to rest for a few days.

When Master Shifu and his family returned to the center, he came to see me after training the next night.

"I heard you helped with the new German man. You ran to help him when others ran away. This is good. This is the Shaolin way. I would like to know more about you. What is your name?"

This was not what I expected. I was relieved I wasn't in trouble.

We talked for over an hour. I showed him some photos on my laptop of my children, my life, my work. He asked me about who I studied Qigong and Traditional Chinese Medicine with and where. He asked about my reason for coming to Yun Tai.

"How do you know about us? We are not the best training center or the most famous, but we are Shaolin. We have a simple life here and strict rules. It is a good life, you will see."

Then he took out two tea bags and told me to prepare and drink the teas during the day for the next two days. He also told me my Shifu would give me the name and address of Tuina (medical massage and bone moving) practitioners in the nearby village who could treat me and help with healing my right side. He asked about my visa and how long I could stay. I told him I intended to stay a total of six months.

He asked if we could have more conversations like this. I happily said, "Yes, thank you. Xie xie"

Then we each said, "Wai an." Goodnight.

The next week children were preparing to leave for their winter and Chinese New Year holidays. I was coming up on the limit of my stay according to the restrictions on my multiple-entry visa, so I would have to leave the country and re-enter. Europeans were able to stay three months in China before having to leave and re-enter. Americans had to leave every two months. I asked around for a place to go where I could continue some form of training while I waited to return.

Many practitioners of Kung Fu and mixed martial arts go to Thailand to train, and some of the Germans and Austrians had done it before. A round trip ticket from where we were in China to Bangkok was not expensive. They went to train in Muay Thai, also known as Thai boxing, as an addition to Sampa, but I decided I would try to increase my flexibility and muscle extension with Yoga and Pilates. They suggested the less touristy island of Koh Phangan.

I searched online and found a place which offered training in both techniques and had a residential unit as well. It was owned by Israelis and named Wonderland.

I sent them an email right away.

# CHAPTER SIX

# Buddhist Smiles

My connections to Thailand started with my Thai roommate at Georgetown University. Her name was Khanith. She was the same year as me but in the College of Arts and Sciences earning her Bachelor of Science in Finance. As the only child of a father who was a medical doctor and a mother who had a lay job with the Catholic church, Khanith was brought up with loving attention and high expectations. Her parents relocated to the Bronx in New York, to be close to their daughter until she finished university.

Khanith and I traveled by train to New York during our Spring holiday in 1973 to meet them. In their small, tidy apartment her mother prepared duck and many Thai delicacies. We were all excited to get to know each other. They educated me more about the history of Siam (the former name for Thailand), the current political groups vying for power in their country, and the importance of the Thai monarchy which had existed through lineage since the 1300s.

Although Khanith's family was Catholic, they incorporated meditation and chants from Thai Buddhism into their spiritual practice. They, like others I met from Indigenous and Buddhist sects, did not see any conflict in believing in both ways of living on this Earth. Thailand reported more than 95% of their population were self-professed Theravada Buddhists in 1972. There were over 30,000 open Buddhist temples in this small country.

The other religions the Thai government recognized were Islam, Christianity, Hinduism, Sikhism and Confucianism. Other religions are tolerated in this land famous for its kindness. Thailand has been known globally as "The Land of Smiles."

After we graduated from Georgetown, Khanith and her family returned to Bangkok, Thailand. I received a few letters from her over the next year or two (this was the 1970s, before the Internet) then lost contact.

Then, one summer while I was living in the Village in New York City. I heard a knock at my door. This meant it was either someone else in our six-floor walk-up, or someone who had been let in from the street.

I approached the apartment door and peeked out the peephole. My heart leapt into my throat. It was Khanith. I hadn't seen her for seven years, but she looked the same to me, smiling as wide as ever. I let her in. We hugged hello. She was concerned to see I was wearing a neck brace and had visible bruises. I had been injured a week before.

"Sawat di," I managed a short hello in Thai. Khanith did a partial bow with her palms pressed together and responded in Thai. Then I brought her over to our couch in my very small, open plan kitchen and living room. We sat close to each other.

"How did you find me?" I asked.

"I have contacts and you are not hard to find with a last name like Munisteri. You're in the telephone book. I'm so glad to see you. But what happened to you?"

"It's a rather long story, but this guy was high on drugs and tried to choke me and throw me out the window in my apartment. Luckily others heard, but he ran away before the police came. I should be fine in a couple of weeks."

"It appears we are both victims of violence. I'm here because I am hoping to get magazines or publishers interested in the work, I've been doing with the hill tribes in Thailand. I brought some photographs we took."

"Wait, Khanith, please. Back up. Tell me what you've been doing since you all left New York."

"When I returned home to Bangkok, an older man who was rising in the Thai military started taking me out. He met my parents and asked my father to give his blessing for us to marry." Khanith turned to look out the window, then continued.

"At first, everything seemed to go smoothly. I have two young daughters with him. But then, I found out he had another woman, and worse, when I asked him about it, he beat me.

Then he questioned me about my work, about my political beliefs, about my religious beliefs. Life became unbearable. He threatened to hurt me and my parents if I tried to leave him with our daughters. I felt desperate.

One weekend he said he was taking our daughters to visit his family. I believed him and was happy to be away from him. However, he did not return. I was very worried for our daughters and called his mother. She told me not to call again. I had a terrible feeling I was going to be in trouble because of my husband.

Military men came to our house. I quickly wrapped a towel around my hair to look like I was in the shower. They told me to pack and come with them. I stalled. I asked them sweetly to please wait out front while I rinse my hair and change. Then I turned on the shower and called my father. He advised me not to go with them but try and escape the back way, but not go anywhere my husband might predict I would go.

I packed one bag quickly and was able to sneak out the back and got a friend to drive me up to the mountains. I had worked there with the Hmong people and other hill tribes. Some of them knew me. There are no phones or electricity up there. They are wary of police or military and would warn me if any came to look for me. But I was so sad to have to leave my daughters and my parents."

I nodded my head and Khanith continued.

"I worked teaching the Hmong children and learning their language. I told just two people I trusted where I was, but I didn't dare contact my parents. They knew it was better if I disappeared for a while. They would try and see my daughters when they could.

I found out my husband had me put on an 'enemy list.' He told people I was speaking against the Monarchy and against the government, which was completely untrue, but I couldn't fight against his tactics. He was too powerful.

One of our mutual friends from Georgetown was in Bangkok trying to contact me last year. She went to the photography studio where I had a colleague she knew. He told her what happened. She gave him money for me to buy a ticket to New York where she thought she could help me. That's how I got here. I have two more weeks. Then I need to return to Thailand."

"Alright, Khanith. Let's see how I can help. First, do you want something to drink? Hot tea or something cold?"

We spent the next five hours discussing possible people and companies to approach for sponsorship of her work. This was in 1980, not that long after the Vietnam War and the secret war in Cambodia and Laos were over. I made phone calls, but no one was interested in helping Khanith or the hill tribes. I told Khanith I would keep trying and she could stay since I had an extra bed and my roommate would not return for another month.

"No, thank you," Khanith replied, "I need to go back to my other friend's apartment. Besides, you need to rest and recover. I'll come again tomorrow afternoon."

"OK, but call me if you need anything. Here is my phone number." I wrote down my landline number. There were no cell phones yet.

"I'm leaving some photos for you. You can show them to the people who might be interested in helping us. If not, you can keep them to remember me by."

The photos were beautiful and in color. I walked Khanith to the door and we arranged to meet again the next day after lunch. I looked out the window to wave as she exited the building and walked back to the subway.

I spent most of that evening on the phone trying to find someone with a connection to National Geographic or Vietnam Veterans who might be able to help. I got a direct line to one of the National Geographic editors, but he only listened for about two minutes and replied that they had their own photographers and writers. Moreover, it wasn't a part of the world they were covering that year.

I slept fitfully both because of my concern for Khanith and on account of the ache in my neck, shoulders and back.

I did dream briefly about the Hill tribes though I'd never been to Thailand. I saw young girls carrying their babies and smoking hand rolled cigarettes and hand-made pipes. The smoke from these pipes obscured their faces and blew up into mine until I woke up.

Khanith returned the next afternoon. I gave her the news of my efforts so far but assured her I would keep trying. She wasn't having any luck either.

She was also worried she might be followed. She thought a Thai man was watching her where she was staying uptown. Khanith worried she might not make it back to Thailand and her daughters.

"Who would have thought our lives would turn like this?" Khanith mused. "We were rising stars, doing well at university, our whole lives ahead of us. We were hoping for someone who would love us and want a family with us. It must not be our destiny. Or maybe we are paying off a karmic debt."

"You are one of the most deeply good people I know, Khanith. I don't believe this is any of your fault. Sometimes we attract predator types or those who want to destroy goodness. It happens to children as well. It's not their fault at all if someone does terrible things to them, is it?"

"No, Joanne, but it depends on your understanding of the wheel of life. Maybe it's why we Thai are more accepting of whatever happens in life. Sometimes I think Buddhism is used as an excuse for not taking action against evil. I'm still thinking about this."

"Me, too. The Bible talks about 'turning the other cheek' but there are acts people do that cannot be ignored in my experience, or they will continue to do grievous harm. Especially to children."

"Yes, I'm so worried about my little daughters. Their father and his family are not good people. Listen, I am giving you this card. This is the name of the studio and photographer I know in Bangkok. If you come to Thailand, find him and you can find me. If something happens to me, he should know."

"Do you think your husband wants you dead, Khanith? Does he have the means to do it without consequences?"

"Yes, to both questions. He could make it that no one ever finds me, and he would tell everyone I ran away from him and our daughters. Pray for me, will you?"

We hugged before Khanith left. I kept the card for many years. I even tried calling the number, but no one could (or would) give me any information about Khanith. I never saw her again.

My next connection was through my friend and apartment mate in Wellington, New Zealand, while I was completing my last years at the New Zealand School of Acupuncture. She was originally from the Philippines, and at one point she was the South Asia director for the NGO Save the Children. She managed the challenging projects for rescuing children after the tsunami in 2004,and relocated to Thailand after 2006. She was based in Bangkok for many years. I emailed her after I made arrangements to train in Koh Phangan.

I left Yun Tai toward the end of January 2019. I packed light and assured my Shaolin Shifus and families I would return in February.

To reach the island of Koh Phangan, I took a short flight from Bangkok, and then a ferry ride to a town near the site of Wonderland. The warmer climate was soothing after the cold winter winds of central China.

I was greeted by a local Thai man and taken to a room with a fan, a large comfortable bed and a private bathroom with hot and cold running water. It

Hmong Children in the hills of Northern Thailand

Indigenous Hill Tribe woman in Thailand

was basic but it felt like luxury. A schedule of classes was posted in each room. I had my choice of which ones and how many I would take in a day. They also had a swimming pool, a buffet style outdoor dining space and a detox section with sauna, massage and colonics. Wi Fi was sporadic, but there were few times I needed to be on email each week.

Further along on the island there were centers for Muay Thai, Kickboxing, and other hard martial arts. They were attended primarily by men. This was yoga and Pilates—softer training. Mostly women stayed at this resort-type training center. It was just what I needed to complete stretching on my right side.

I noticed in the first yoga classes that my right arm already had greater range of motion. I was in less pain doing the movements and holding positions. I was the only American there at the time. There were women from Eastern Europe, Russia, Australia and Israel, and locals from the community who came for a meal, or a class or two.

We all ate together, sat in meditation together, and worked out together in the comfortable training halls. A young woman from an Eastern European country struck up a conversation with me at dinner. It turned out we had much in common in our love of performing arts and opera. We heard about a Buddhist monastery a few kilometers inland and decided we would hike and spend the day there. We also heard there were monks at this monastery who were healers and could guide us. That piqued my interest. A few days later, after an early morning rain, we headed out.

As it turns out, the young woman, my hiking partner for the day, worked for NATO. She spoke at least three languages and was quite tall. Two of my strides made one of hers, but I was keen to see this remote temple.

It took over an hour of walking in the heat before we saw the golden tops of buildings peeking up over the forest's growth. We soon spotted a sign in Thai and English. We'd made it to the front gate. No one was around.

We followed a path to a long stairway that wound up a steep hill. At the top were two dragon statues and a small building where a few monks were sitting in prayer. We were careful to be as quiet as possible.

After we completed our walk around the building and took a few minutes to admire the view at the top of the hill, one of the monks rose from his sitting position and slowly approached us. He spoke some English. After a short conversation he motioned for us to follow him.

The area near their altar smelled of incense and there were chimes above us tinkling with high pitched sounds in the breeze. We sat in silent meditation with them for about

Top of the stairway to the Buddhist temple. Photo by author in 2019.

15 minutes and then each of us had a private session sitting opposite the head monk.

He examined my hands carefully, looked at my tongue and eyes, then closed his own eyes and contemplated. He told me I would be going back to study in China (I hadn't mentioned this to him) and to be braver to "trust what you see." He reminded me it was a gift to help others. He also said not to give up.

"Your family is with you here." He pointed to his heart and the sky. "You won't have to suffer much longer in this life."

I thanked him and sat a little longer in quiet meditation and prayer. Then we both descended the long staircases down the hill in silence. We saw a donation box and placed our cash in gratitude. After walking around the grounds, we decided to start our hike back although it was the hottest part of the day.

We didn't speak much on our trek back, partly because of the searing heat and humidity and partly because we were each pondering what had been said to us.

I thought about my family, my daughter and her meditation retreats in Thailand and her apparent affection for this country.

Thinking back over my ex-husband's love of Thailand, I realized it was probably for the partying and the easy way to procure sex without being accountable or getting caught.

He always found an excuse to route his travels for guiding through Thailand, even sent us postcards from Koh Samui and Bangkok.

Yes, some of my family was with me in spirit here.

"Want to go into town for a while? We can get a taxi."

My companion was eager to do some shopping before she left Wonderland. I obliged. When

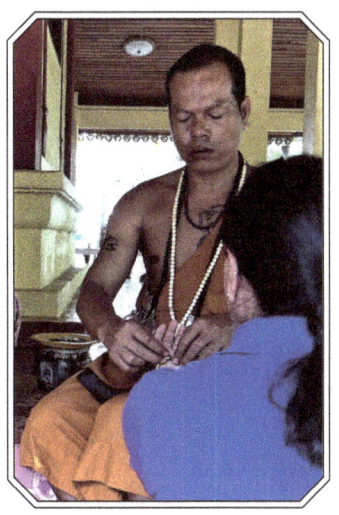

Buddhist Monk in Dragon Temple Koh Phangan 2019

we arrived in the early evening, there was a bonfire on the beach and tourists (I assumed) from different countries were playing music, drinking and dancing. It was a full moon.

We agreed to meet at a central location after two hours, then each went our separate ways.

As I walked, I couldn't help noticing a group of about nine young children in a spot on the beach. None of them looked related, and there were two huge, muscled men as well as two older women who spoke Russian, minding them. Something didn't seem right about the situation. The children looked thin and stressed and were told to sit down on large towels. Some were drinking sodas, but they hardly spoke or played together. I reckoned their ages to be between seven and twelve. Something about this group seemed strange to me. My internal radar went off. Maybe these children were being 'displayed' to be sold.

Regrettably, thousands of people come to Thailand every month seeking sex and other forms of debauchery, since the "Land of Smiles" is also the "Land of Sleaze." Thailand's beautiful children, beautiful scenery and nefarious criminal networks combine to make the Golden Triangle area a hell on earth for those trafficked, imprisoned in the life of a sex worker slave, taken away from their families and homes to be sold as a 'product' or 'package'. Drugs are also integral to this trade.

Pedophilia, child rape, child kidnapping, child torture, child exploitation in all forms *is never not a crime,* yet these crimes are growing globally. Most people don't know that the USA is documented as the number-one consumer of child sex in all its forms, and the number-one destination for child sex trafficking and child sex slavery in the world.

And while we may be on retreat or on vacation in different parts of the world as well as in North America, it doesn't mean we can turn a blind eye to this crime,or excuse those we know among our family and friends who participate in 'sex tourism' at home or abroad. Doing nothing is a form of complicity.

But how do you prove it, and who do you tell? Who can you trust to help the victims? Who can be trusted not to be tempted to profit off them? And who is not threatened or controlled by nefarious criminal networks? Corruption is everywhere.

There are numerous non-government organizations (NGOs) in Thailand working against child sex trafficking and other labor industries that exploit children.

But you do have to be careful that the NGO is actually legitimate and not using money for other purposes, or worse, not taking in vulnerable children only to use and "disappear" them again.

*The UN and UNICEF programs are not to be trusted.* I have witnessed firsthand United Nations workers bragging about being able to procure "very young children as escorts" in a number of countries including in Afghanistan and Ukraine. There have been documented cases in a number of countries of supervisory UN officials and UNICEF program managers involved in child and sexual abuse. Incredible as it may seem, often the whistleblowers on these crimes were prosecuted *and not the United Nations officials who were the perpetrators.*

The child sex trafficking problem is endemic in Thailand and much of Southeast Asia. The criminal networks processing and transiting children from other countries to Thailand and neighboring countries *is increasing.* Children, tragically, can be ordered, traded and bought on the darknet. Children from Eastern Europe, Scandinavia, the Middle East and North America are 'ordered' then 'transferred' to Thailand.

Internet users post children "for sale" under codified descriptions. They label different ethnicities, ages and genders but substitute the word child, branding children as different animals, fruits, food, furniture types to disguise the real 'products'.

"According to the Ministry of Social Development and Human Security, numbers of foreign children being trafficked *to Thailand* for sexual exploitation is on the increase. They are trafficked from neighboring countries such as Cambodia, China (Yunnan Province), Laos, Myanmar and Vietnam while Thai children are trafficked into sex businesses abroad, such as in Japan and Australia, via Malaysia and Hong Kong. For internal trafficking, the majority of the trafficked victims are hill tribe girls aged around 12 to 16 years old from the north and northeastern part of the country.

They are usually sent to closed brothels, which operate under prison-like conditions. Women and children, mainly from Thailand, are trafficked to countries in the Middle East such as Saudi Arabia and the United Arab Emirates to be prostitutes or brides." www.ecpat.org/wp-content/uploads/legacy/Factsheet_Thailand.pdf

Internally I was struggling to figure out what to do. I decided to send an email to my friend who was working in Bangkok with NGOs. But she sent back a message saying she was in the Philippines to visit her family for two weeks. We would miss each other, and for now, I would have to wait.

As in other times in my life, being on my own, it was not prudent for either my own safety or that of the children I sought to help, if I were to try to investigate or report on what I suspected was illegal and illicit activity. Especially as a *farang*—a foreigner, specifically a Caucasian foreigner, I was at a disadvantage. I didn't know the language and who to trust with a report.

However, at least by writing and exposing even a sliver of the huge, tenacious and evil industry child sex trafficking has become, I hope to keep this issue in the forefront of people's minds. I endeavor to prod those who have the authority and power to prosecute perpetrators and predators both in the flesh, and who operate online.

We need to be vigilant in protecting children in whichever way and in whatever capacity we can.

For the rest of my time in Koh Phangan, I concentrated on getting as strong, flexible and ready as possible for my next two months at Yun Tai. I avoided the town and spent my time in the training hall, the hills and the pool.

By the end of my four weeks of training, detoxing in warm weather, and working in different modalities that stretched me, I was keen to return to Yun Tai with a renewed commitment to the Shaolin form of training in China.

# CHAPTER SEVEN

# Yun Tai Encore

I returned to China from Bangkok via Kunming. The airport was packed with Chinese coming and going for the Chinese New Year holidays.

Once again, I was met by a driver from the Yun Tai International Martial Arts Training Center at the airport in Zhengzhou. He drove into sunrise.

The weather was still freezing. Snow frosted the courtyard, trees and buildings. It was early in the morning and some Shaolin were out sweeping the snow off the cement with their bamboo brush brooms in time for morning muster and workout. They looked up when I came to the gate.

A broad inner smile filled me with a quiet joy as I made my way across the courtyard and up the six flights of stairs to my room. No doors were locked at Yun Tai. Everything was as I left it. Quickly, I changed into my uniform and

Bamboo brush broom
at Yun Tai center,
2019.

mentally prepared for my first day back to training. I felt strong and ready.

Children ran down the stairs chattering and excited. I jogged to my place in line and waited for the Shifus. They didn't have on warmer jackets, just the thin black track suits they always wore. There were very few international students. Most departed during the Chinese New Year long holiday. The Shifus did not say "welcome back" but simply nodded at me. We were consolidated into two groups. My Shifu was on vacation. The Master Shifu said we were to be combined with the Kung Fu group for ten days. My eyes widened. This was much harder physical training than Qigong and Tai Chi. They did more acrobatics, weights, running and fighting. I swallowed hard.

"Three times around...go," Master Shifu commanded after we had stretched and done short warm ups as a group. We jogged on the cement now cleared of snow. After the third lap we paused at the stairs going up to the training hall.

"Push-ups to the training hall. Go." This meant doing push-ups on each step. The steps were freezing. We finished and stood in rows on the mats awaiting further instructions.

"Fifty sit-ups. Go! Stand. Fifty jumping jacks. Go! Spider crawls. Go! Twenty push-ups. Go. Stand. Down the mat, outside kicks. Go. Down the mat, inside kicks. Go. Sprints down the mat. Go. Again. Lie down, scissor kicks. Go"

This went on for the first hour. This was the warm up session before breakfast. I was panting hard when I approached Shifu once we were dismissed.

"Ni hao, Shifu. I'm not sure if I can do the next sessions of Kung Fu. Maybe I'm too old now to keep up with the fighting exercises."

Shifu looked into my eyes for a moment.

"I know you can. It is you who think you can't. I watched you for two months. You can do more now. It's not your age. It's your mind and body. You will continue with the Kung Fu group this week. Go eat."

"Xie xie, Shifu." I bowed to him in the martial arts way, hand to fist in front of my heart.

Yes, maybe it was just in my mind. Maybe it was just what I thought I knew from the media, from societal constructs about women in their sixties, from my own misconceptions about training. I was open to trying. Actually, if I were to stay for my planned next two months, I would have no choice. The Shifus were the masters here. Only they made these decisions. It was a warrior society. They had trained effectively for over five thousand years. If he thought I was capable, I was capable. I would give it my all. My arm and whole body were stronger and more flexible after my first months of training with the Shaolin. How much more could I improve given another two months? It was up to me.

In the dining hall the main cook half nodded when he saw me. He came outside on his breaks to watch us train. He usually maintained a poker face. He brought out the huge metal cauldron and, with the help of other staff, poured in the steaming hot cabbage and chicken broth with noodles. He served it to us using a long-handled soup ladle, the stem of which could double as a staff. A weapon in his skilled hands. He was a big man who had done Sampa in his youth. He had a booming voice which he used daily to chase away enthusiastic, hungry young teenagers who clamored to his window for food.

The second session was grueling. We partnered up and sat on each other's legs to push them further down to the ground and stretch our muscles. We did bridges or backbends, and I tried to 'walk over' but kept falling down. Then we did minutes of fast and slow punches and kicks to the sound of Shifu counting in Mandarin. Often, he would stop at a number and go backwards. We would need to pay close attention to his instructions.

Just when I thought we were approaching the end of an exercise because the count was near ten, he would stop and repeat the number eight, "Ba" in Chinese, then go backwards and get "stuck" at "wu" (five). It was almost amusing except my muscles were screaming for this to stop.

Then back into the horse stance for more punches and kicks coordinated with sounds as we struck with our limbs. Sound is used as a tactic for both releasing more energy and startling your opponent (or enemy) to catch them off guard. Certain sounds can release different emotions. There is a whole science to this in Chinese medicine and martial arts.

For example: "Ssss" releases anger. "Eee" releases surprise, delight. "Ah" releases wonder and relaxes the diaphragm. "Oh" releases anxiety. "Huh, huh" is a sound to show aggression, and "Eh, eh" is used as a question, to interrogate.

The shortest and smallest children could already project their voices across the courtyard using these exercises. Some of us had 'constricted voices'. We needed to shout from our Dan Tian at the center of our body near our navel, but deep inside. This 'gate' released more energy/ Qi and grounded the sound so we didn't just screech from our throat. It was liberating, and the sound resonated throughout my body. Long ago I practiced similar exercises while in the performing arts to be able to sing and project on stage. I was thirsty for more sound.

At lunch time I ran upstairs to unpack a few things I'd brought for certain people I'd connected with on the staff. I'd purchased a few Swiss chocolate bars to give as presents for New Year's and Valentine's Day to certain workers at the center. They were not allowed to receive tips or most other gifts, but often accepted small food items.

I learned how to say "Happy New Year" in Mandarin: Xin nian kuai le.

It was one of the few times gifts were exchanged. When I tried my Mandarin greeting with the cook and presented him with a dark chocolate bar, he looked surprised. He gave me the martial arts bow and accepted it. Later, I saw him take it outside and try a piece. He savored it then rewrapped the chocolate and put it in his apron pocket. I was happy he liked it. At the end of our last training and after supper, he mounted his motorbike, nodded at me, then rode home.

The evening session was especially chilly in the training hall. One thing we learned right away was to never say you were cold. To do so meant one of the Shifus would find more exercises or work to "keep you warm."

We were no longer permitted to turn on heaters in our rooms. They were centrally controlled after an incident happened that resulted in collective punishment.

The incident involved one of the Kung Fu trainees, a tall, graceful young college student from the Philippines. Her mother was Filipino and her father was Norwegian. She was six feet tall and very beautiful. And she knew it. Her nickname was The Gazelle. She was studying international finance at a Chinese university but came to Yun Tai over the holidays to do some martial arts training.

The day before she was to leave, she decided she wanted to be warm and turned on the heater in her room for the

In front of the statue of Confucius February 14, 2019
Yun Tai International Martial Arts Training Center,
Henan province, China.
Photo by Shifu.

evening, leaving it on all night and into the morning. The maintenance man, who was an elder Shaolin, felt the heat coming from her room. Her roommate had apparently gone along with this waste of electricity and not stopped her, or reported it. As a result, at the next meeting after breakfast, we were all called to line up outside.

Master Shifu and the maintenance man stood in front of us and asked who had their heater turned on all night when it was known we were only permitted two hours. They knew who it was, but she had to admit it. No one responded. He asked again. This time she stepped forward. She knew she was leaving that afternoon.

Shifu calmly explained why this was an egregious offense and why she would now be remembered as the trainee who caused the new policy. He stated, "From now on, the heaters will be controlled by maintenance." They could no longer trust the trainees to monitor themselves according to the looser guidelines. It would be a communal consequence.

We did remember 'The Gazelle' every night of that winter.

In the last part of February, we shared the training hall on freezing days with the high school students. They were rehearsing for Spring Kung Fu performances. They would look at us training and keep a neutral face, but we knew they could outdo us in every way. Most had been training since they were six or seven years old. We could see them training outside in the afternoon, doing acrobatics on concrete and practicing their forms in perfect unison.

It was an inspiring and beautiful sight to me. They were harmony in motion.

Master Shifu and I would have conversations at night after the last meeting. He asked many questions about the West. I answered as best I could. By this time, I was also treating some of the international students with acupuncture and herbs. There was no doctor on site. I prepared a First Aid kit for both the kitchen and training hall.

I also translated a list of rules the Shifus wanted international trainees to abide by. I wrote up the list in English at their request. They were posted in our dorm and in the training hall. They included rules about no photos or videos without permission. It was becoming a problem since younger international students were posting on social media sites. The Chinese Communist Party (CCP-Chinese government) monitored all media, and these posts brought Yun Tai onto their radar. This would prove detrimental to their community in the months and years to come.

Master Shifu called me out one morning after breakfast.

"Today, I have a special teacher for you. He was one of my masters. He is visiting and I told him about you. He wants to see you do the forms."

"Thank you, Shifu." I was both nervous and eager.

I did the standing forms I was taught. He asked me to do them again slower, then faster. This master watched me carefully with no outward expression. As I began the forms a third time, he came over to me and grasped my right wrist. He circled my injured arm in a wide circle. Then he showed me another way to execute the movements with circular motion. It made an immediate difference. The two Shifus spoke to each other while observing me. My master Shifu came over.

"Shifu says you need to perfect this form. He worked on this form over eight years once. This form will release the pain more. You will soon be able to move your right arm as before—if you practice perfectly. Only perfect practice makes it perfect. Understand?"

I replied "Yes, Shifu" in Mandarin. My vocabulary and understanding were increasing with time. I enjoyed practicing my Chinese, as my Shifu enjoyed practicing his English.

Practicing my form was also becoming enjoyable. The adjustment the visiting Shifu gave me helped me progress to the next level. I did well on the biweekly tests where we had to perform in front of all the Shifus and international students.

Shifu asked me if I could teach English in the late afternoon to some of the children, their teachers, and a few of the Shifus. In exchange I would not be charged extra for my single room for the next two months. This was an opportunity to get to know more of the Shaolin community. I was happy to oblige.

A classroom was designated as my English classroom. I shared it with the math teacher. I taught five afternoons a week. The class was more than full with two teachers, children aged 7-17, a few Shifus and the one Russian girl who was both my interpreter and a student. She was my trilingual assistant. We worked well team-teaching even though we were 50 years apart in age.

Elder Shaolin monk walking with a cell phone in Yun Tai hills.

In February 2018, the President of China's Communist Party removed the restriction of the president governing for two terms. Xi Jinping was declared "President for Life." Concurrently, a "social credit" system run by AI logarithms created by Google whose parent company was the California based, American Alphabet Inc company; was installed in major cities in China.

Surveillance cameras installed in public buildings, courtyard spaces, main dormitory buildings facing the courtyard ran 24 hours a day, or at least as long as the electricity was working. The privacy of Shaolin life up in the mountains was being invaded. This was a different type of enemy they weren't prepared to fight.

Typical school classroom
at Yun Tai Martial Arts Center 2019.

Music and messages from the ruling Community Party were displayed on the screen during the day. The bells signaling breaks were replaced by harsh electronic muzak with child-like voices singing phrases and maxims from the CCP. These clashed with the sounds of nature that once set the rhythm of life on the mountain. The sacred atmosphere of Yun Tai was submerged. This was the intention. Shaolin were known for being an independent and strong society with their unique culture and traditions.

The Shifus announced two trips for the international students in March 2019. One was to Tanpu Canyon, and the other was to the famous Shaolin Monastery at Wuru peak in the Songshan mountain range in Dengfeng. This

Screen mounted on main dormitory in March 2019.
High school students in line outside
at Yun Tai Martial Arts Center

was the world-famous Shaolin Buddhist temple and monastery.

Originally established in 477 A.D., it retained its independence and survived through numerous emperors, dynasties, and Mao's cultural revolution, until the year 2000, when the government started to infringe on its activities. In 2000, they were forced to open their doors to tourists.

In 2010, the monastery, all the buildings and grounds were declared a United Nations (UNESCO) World Heritage site. This promoted the Shaolin to a higher global profile.

Theatrical performances by Shaolin monks in training became part of the program at Dengfeng.

In August 2018, the CCP demanded they raise the CCP flag over the monastery, and accept the Communist party's choice for Abbots. This was the beginning of the end of the true Shaolin way of life at the centuries-old monastery. It became a kind of commercialized theme park instead of a sacred and serious Buddhist site for the highly trained, sanctified Shaolin warrior monks. Nonetheless, it was certainly worth visiting. We traveled there by bus.

Sword shop-Songshan Dengfeng, March 2019.

My Tai Chi and Qigong Shifu sat by me in the theatre at Dengfeng. He pointed out which moves were changed for an audience. When he was younger, he had performed there until he broke vertebrae in his back after a fall on cement during night practice.

"It was my fault. I didn't check the mats were secure and they separated. I landed on the cement. My chance for performing was over. But I like teaching. I meet many people like you. I learn very much."

During the next part of the show my Shifu pointed out the line of performers.

"See. No power. No true Qi. Just show." I could sense what he meant. Having seen the real Shaolin, I noted there was a grounded grace and inner power that permeated and radiated in their being. These performers had the outward appearance and definitely the skill and flexibility to demonstrate these movements, but the inner power and energy of Qi was missing.

We stayed for hours, walking about the grounds, going into temples and sitting together at a restaurant for a meal. There were thousands of tourists but most of them looked like they came from other parts of China. When trainees would jog by or do exercises in various courtyards on the grounds, people would stand and stare as if they were looking at exotic creatures in a living zoo. It was a very different environment from Yun Tai. I felt fortunate we would be returning to the other side of the mountain that evening.

We returned after midnight and were told we still had to be on time at the first roll call the next morning at 6:00 am. The wind had died down, so I opened my window and looked up at the stars for a time before going to sleep. I was fulfilling one of my life's wishes. I had seen the original Shaolin monastery in Dengfeng and I was training with actual Shaolin Warriors in Yun Tai. It took many decades to get here, but I would soon have my 66th birthday at this international martial arts training center. How blessed I was.

There was a hint of Spring in the air the next morning. It seemed all of us were recharged after our trip to the monastery. Our training was more rigorous than ever, but our minds and bodies were ready to meet the new demands.

On Sundays, we had a few hours to go to the nearby village or to take an hour or more bus ride to Jiazuo. I went into the village for therapeutic massages and tuina (bone and muscle moving, similar to osteopathy). I had been going for months to a clinic run by a Shaolin family known to be from a lineage of healers. My Shifu had given me their address and now others from our group would go with me as well.

This family lived toward the back of a rabbit warren of twisting alleys and doorways. The father was almost blind, but he saw with his hands and other senses. He was masterful at finding where your muscles were tight and sore. I tried to get him as my practitioner whenever I went.

He had four sons. Three of them were also massage and tuina practitioners. Everyone was treated in one room on massage tables quite close to each other. No partitions. You could hear and see the other patients. There was one wood-burning stove and they made tea from the kettle of hot water on top of it. The mother or one of the son's wives (the family's daughters in law) would greet whomever came in and take their money for treatment. They charged us the "foreigner's" rate, about $10 USD for a treatment which usually lasted at least 30 minutes, sometimes up to an hour. Locals paid less.

Another family member drove a tuk tuk taxi. When we were finished, they would call him and he would drive us back to Yun Tai, or back to the center of the village if we needed to do some shopping.

The village was not large and had very basic places to shop. People sold meat from the trunk of their car, had stalls selling breads and pastries, fruits and vegetables, or CCS (cheap Chinese stuff) like plastics, housewares and clothes.

There was music blasting over loudspeakers into the street, and some sellers would shout over the music calling us to "buy here" in the local dialect. Local people would openly stare at us. No tourists ever came to this part of China. I learned everyone knew who "the Kung Fu students" were and where we lived.

One place I was introduced to in my first month at Yun Tai was a shop that sold freshly ground peanut and sesame butter as well as their special apiary honey. You bought the size jar you wanted and watched as they poured the peanuts into a large grinder that squeezed out fresh peanut butter. The honey could be bought with part of the honeycomb or

Freshly ground peanut butter, honey, and sesame butter
family run business in the village near Yun Tai,
March 2019.

"pure." It was all delicious. We were allowed to keep a few
food items in our room. My go to treat was spoonfuls of
peanut butter with honey. Energy foods.

The end of March 2019, brought high winds and the last
of the snows. Children reveled in the high drifts and made
a huge snowman right beside the entrance to the dining
facility. They were pleased with it and put stones as the
eyes and created a mouth. When the bell rang for lunch,
they skipped inside for hot soup.

A few of the new students who came after the Chinese New Year and who were evidently not from Shaolin families went over to the snowman. These boys were about twelve and not yet in shape or integrated into the Shaolin culture. They started tearing down the snowman, making snowballs out of its huge snow belly and throwing snow everywhere. What they didn't know was that there were a number of Shaolin men watching them do this. They stomped down on the snowman, laughing, then went to eat without a care.

As lunch was finishing and we were all washing our bowls and chopsticks at the communal sinks, some of the young, strong Shifus went over and pulled out the boys who destroyed the little children's snowman. They drove them forward outside to where the last of the snowman remained.

An elder Shaolin came over and started speaking in a strong voice to them. We watched from up above in the training hall. I don't know what they said, but the next thing we saw was all those boys down doing push-ups in the snow and the Shifu's counting. It was a just consequence. Bullying, especially to those younger or more vulnerable, was a major offense in the book of Shaolin.

As the weather became milder, the flowers and trees blossomed around Yun Tai. You could feel the "Spring fever" energy wafting through the children and staff. My body was getting used to the training and was re-forming. I observed that anyone who came and stayed at least a month would improve. If you stayed more than three months, the progress was apparent to everyone. If you could stay six months or longer, the change would be longer lasting.

An American woman in her late twenties arrived just before the end of March 2019. She was at least 70 pounds overweight and brought far too many suitcases. We couldn't believe she had any training but she loudly proclaimed she had been training "for years" and wanted to do Kung Fu.

The first few days she was breathless, and like many who came before her, she vomited after the first session. She kept stopping during exercises and the Shifus would come over and tell her to try again. They were quite patient. Before her first week ended, I was called to her room at 5:00 in the morning. Her roommate ran to get me and said she was "having a heart attack." I rushed in. She wasn't but she was having a panic attack and was very pale, shaking and breathless. I asked her if I could put in a few needles. She nodded with her eyes rolling back in their sockets. Her roommate ran to get Master Shifu.

I rolled her on her side and placed a few more needles just as Master Shifu entered. He looked concerned. I asked this woman a few questions about her medical history. It turned out she had a heart condition. She had it since she was a child but hadn't put it on her application form because she said she hadn't had palpitations or other symptoms in years.

Shifu heard this and looked at me. "We need to take her to the hospital right away. You come with me, please."

I agreed and went to change. Her roommate helped her change into suitable clothes. I rushed back to her room and together we helped her down the six flights of stairs. When the car arrived, I sat in the back with the American woman, and Master Shifu sat up front. We each asked her a few more questions about her life, medical history, medications, her insurance and training over the hour ride to the hospital. If this woman died, it would be a terrible liability for the Shifus and Yun Tai training center in addition to the tragedy for this woman and her family.

When we got to the hospital, they asked for money since she was a foreigner. She hadn't brought any and at this point she told us she was on welfare back in the US. Shifu paid the receptionist and we were directed upstairs to the Cardiology department. Because she was obviously a foreigner, she was taken in ahead of a long line of patients. I felt embarrassed as a fellow countrywoman. The Shaolin had almost no money by American standards, and the other patients waiting in the hospital were obviously very ill, yet they were disregarded and we were ushered forward.

The hospital staff did a number of tests. The hospital was clean and had a lot of modern equipment. They determined she had a small hole in her heart and said she should consider an operation back in the States. She was told to rest and take blood pressure medication. The Shifu translated.

When we returned to Yun Tai she went to her room and slept. Master Shifu spoke to me privately.

179

Front entrance Jiazuo hospital. Henan Province, China 2019.

"We cannot let her continue here," he said. "She needs to return to America and have this operation. She needs to work on her health if she wants to continue training."

"I agree. Shifu, have you thought about having a medical form with the application for training? I can create one for you to use. It seems there have been a number of cases where trainees coming from overseas have serious medical conditions, they didn't tell you about."

"Yes. Make the form. You can help the American woman get ready to leave. I will explain to her if she doesn't understand."

"I can do both, Shifu." He thanked me and I went to her room. The other international students were training. The dormitory was quiet.

"Look, I'm sorry but you need to return home. The Shifus cannot be responsible for you here and you cannot continue training. I can help you search for a flight online."

"No, I'm not going back. It's not that serious. I can find another training center. Maybe in Dengfeng. I hear they aren't as strict and you only train five days a week. Better food, too."

I tried reasoning with her but she was adamant about not leaving China. Master Shifu let her rest for three more days then had the driver take her to the airport despite her protests. We heard she went to another training center outside of Dengfeng. It was her choice.

One week later, Master Shifu came to me and asked if I would like to see state schools in Jiazuo. He had permission to take a few of us to visit. It was a chance to see inside public education and for them to see a few foreigners. We were to dress in our uniforms. They hosted an English club in the schools and we would eat lunch with them. I eagerly agreed. We were told we could not take our phones, nor take any photos. I expected this restriction.

We went to three schools, one elementary school and two high schools. In each school I was asked to do a few minutes teaching for the students. I taught some basic phrases in English and a song. The classes were large, 40-50 students to one teacher, but the students were very attentive and polite. Each school we visited had more than one thousand students.

The school buildings were run down and painted a bilious green and white. There were posters of Xi Jinping in the halls, and each classroom had long wooden tables and benches for the students. They used large green chalkboards and each teacher had an assistant. There were about as many male teachers as female teachers and more boys than girls in the schools. The students were not as free as in Yun Tai in terms of being able to run, jump, play and talk together. The day was completely structured. They used books and notebooks. I didn't see any computers except in the administration building and the teacher common room.

The English club was well attended, and both the students and teachers went out of their way to practice their English and host us. There were four of us trainees and Master Shifu. One young woman from Spain, one man from Austria, and one young man from Germany, and myself. We all spoke English to the school children.

The city of Jiazuo was filled with box-like high-rises. Most families lived in these apartment buildings. There were few green spaces for children to play or people to walk but you did see people of all ages practicing their Tai Chi forms almost anywhere there was space.

Spring was alive even in the congested air of the city. Once again, I felt relieved to be going back up the mountain to Yun Tai.

Inside the walls of Yun Tai Training Center Spring, 2019. Photo by author

At the end of March, the entire school and training center had an awards ceremony. Once a year, students and trainees were recognized for special achievements. A stage was constructed outside. A panel of staff and representatives from the Chinese government council along with all the Shifus sat in front. Over a microphone, they announced the awardees starting with the youngest class.

One of the littlest boys came over and wanted to sit by me. He pulled up his sleeve and showed me a picture he had drawn with a red marker on his forearm. I almost cried. My son, Denali, had done the same when he was about that age. This little boy was one of the orphans that lived and trained at Yun Tai. He pushed his seat closer and we tried to talk to each other with my limited Mandarin.

"You have a new friend," one of the Swiss trainees commented. I was smiling.

The kindergarten teacher came over and scolded the little boy for leaving his assigned spot. He almost cried but stopped himself by lowering his head and covering his face with one hand. When he put his head up his face was neutral. At five or six years old, he already displayed such self-control. I waved goodbye to him as he was taken back to sit with his class.

One of the young French women trainees had told me months ago that she felt she "had been here before" and that she was "returning in this lifetime to continue her Shaolin training." She posed the question to me, "Do you think we've all been here before?"

I replied truthfully, "I don't know." But her question provoked me to think more about reincarnation. When this little boy showed me his forearm for a moment, I thought...what if my son is reincarnated here? He died on the Chinese side of K2 Mountain. He had started Shaolin training in Oakland. Who knows?

I was daydreaming while watching the presentations when suddenly one of my training mates tapped me on the shoulder. "They called your name. You need to go up there."

I was startled. I walked up slowly and Master Shifu presented me with a certificate of honor. Then he bowed to me while giving the martial arts greeting.

Award ceremony at Yun Tai Center courtyard.
March 2019.

When I returned to my seat, I opened my red velvet folder and read the citation. Some of my training mates came over to look. I was stunned. Everyone knew I was one of the least proficient in martial arts though I had definitely progressed, but the young ones were physically much more adept.

After the ceremonies concluded we all went to the dining facility for lunch.

On the way, a few of the Chinese high school girls paused and bowed and gave me the martial arts greeting. To me, this was an honor. I was grinning on the inside as I returned the greeting to them. After lunch I ran upstairs. In my room was a vase of flowers with a personal note from Shifu and the two teachers I had in my English class. They thanked me for my contributions to their training center and to their students. I was deeply touched.

It was approaching the time when my visa needed to be renewed or I would need to return home via New Zealand. I had to make a decision soon. If I stayed another two months, I might not have enough time to visit New Zealand and my daughter in the States before starting my new job back in Kurdistan, Iraq. I decided to meditate on the choice.

Part of training included meditation most mornings after breakfast and one day a week of voluntary meditation with Buddhist teachings. Only the Tai Chi and Qigong students were required to do meditation. I enjoyed sitting in meditation.

Award given to author by the Shifus at Yun Tai in March 2019.

My mind was clearer afterward. After Tai Chi and Qigong practice, it was plain to me I needed to go home via New Zealand for my book tour as planned, and then return to Texas to see family before departing again for Iraq. It would be my second time working in the north, in Kurdistan.

Master Shifu and I continued our talks at night a few times a week. I told him of my decision to leave Yun Tai when my visa was up for renewal in April. He agreed and added, "You have more work to do out in the world, but you are always welcome back here. You have helped many people. We will remember you."

My right arm was restored to more than 95% use without residual pain. I had almost full mobility in all directions. I was stronger, fitter and calmer. As my Shifu had observed, "When you come here, you have no power. Now you have little power."

To have 'power' is very important for the Shaolin, and from what I understand, in Chinese society. There are many types of power, though we have only one word for it in English.

I learned so much in the months of training. My time at Yun Tai provided a renewed admiration and respect for the Shaolin as well as a glimpse of mainstream Chinese society. It was almost two different worlds: the world inside the walls and community of the Shaolin at Yun Tai International Martial Arts Training Center, and the world outside.

It was also contrasting worlds between China and the Western countries I knew and had lived in for most of my life. At times it was hard to believe we were on the same planet. China was the most exotic place and the people were the most different I had ever experienced. Moreover, I knew I had just peered into their culture, language and way of life.

Even if you lived your entire life with the Shaolin, you would not know everything there is to know about their traditions and training. You would have to spend many lifetimes to truly delve into the depths of their world.

Shifu gave permission for me to have a photo taken at one end of Yun Tai where a row of international flags representing the international trainees who had come to the center over the years waved in the wind. I gave the martial arts greeting and farewell.

I would be sorry to leave, but leave I must.

# CHAPTER EIGHT

# Zumba in Ankawa

Ankawa is a particular section of Erbil, Iraq. It is the Christian area. All sorts of Orthodox and ancient sects of Christianity coexist in the small portion of the city. The Catholic church is strong, and their Bishop Warda is a stalwart, compassionate and tireless worker for his congregation and the wider community. He proved himself under fire during the cruel and horrific siege by Daesh, otherwise known as ISIS.

In Ankawa, you hear the languages of the Bible spoken in everyday life. Assyrian, Aramaic, Chaldean, various dialects of both plus the official Arabic and Kurdish languages. You can hear the sweet Lebanese accent or the harsher Syrian and Iraqi accents of Arabic, and at times,

Russian, French or English. Even Armenians and Indians lived in this sector.

The first morning after I arrived to Ankawa, I opened the gate to see a male peacock spreading his plumage and his peahen prancing next to him. A remarkable sight early on a winter morning. An elder man next door came out in his bathrobe. He watched them for a few minutes, then turned to me. We smiled hello to each other.

To me, receiving a peacock's greeting at my new accommodation was a positive sign. Incredibly, the first time I arrived to Kabul, Afghanistan, in 2014, a peacock was strutting on the entranceway as I approached my housing at the American University of Afghanistan (AUA). The coincidence could only be a sign.

Over the next few weeks, I discovered more about this fascinating town of about 35,000. No mosques in our quarter, no calls to prayer, but in their place were church bells, monasteries, and you see nuns from time to time. If you cross over the highway, it is very different environment. There, people often don't know or won't speak Arabic, just Sorani Kurdish. Shops aren't permitted to sell alcohol as they are in Ankawa, and the people dress differently. Most women wear a hijab, a scarf covering their hair, and do not show their arms or legs. I felt more constricted in Erbil city. There is a sense of freedom in Ankawa, in spite of the recent wars. Ankawa is more a community of neighborhoods than a strictly planned city. There are no street signs within the neighborhoods. No postal service to

Peacock across the street in Ankawa, Iraq 2017.

homes. No streetlights. They have their own "security" akin to neighborhood watch and small militias.

Children are everywhere playing outside, riding bicycles, going to church with their families, running over to the shops to pick up something for their mothers or themselves. People look out for each other here out of necessity. There are Maronite Lebanese who patrol at night giving the neighborhood I live in the nickname "Little Beirut". The Catholic University in Erbil (CUE) bank is adjacent to a Lebanese bank. The Assyrian Catholics and Christians co-exist with the Kurds and even the Israeli military (mostly females) who train the Peshmerga fighting force here.

There are Muslim Kurds, Christian and Jewish Kurds. The Kurdish Peshmerga military units, both female and male,

Front of refugee camp in Ankawa,
Iraq 2018.

are known as a fierce and effective force against Daesh/
ISIS and Al Qaeda. Peshmerga translates to "those who
face/confront death."

Everywhere are reminders of the wars. War with Iran,
which is only a few hours away; war with the United States
and its allies; war with Daesh/ISIS. Infrastructure is in
disrepair. There are two large refugee camps directly south
of CUE university, and on the outskirts of town. The largest
is outside Mosul. Catholic charities built and staff most of
these refugee camps.

Electricity is unreliable, and in some places non-existent.
Water is restricted, and clean drinking water needs to be
purchased. Water from the tap is a light brown most days
and toxic to drink or cook with. Water for a shower is
cold in the winter and hot in the summer. Water tanks are

Water rations for children at Mosul refugee camp, Iraq 2018.

usually placed on the outside top levels of a building. The water temperature is only a few degrees different than the outside temperature. Clean water is a precious commodity in Kurdistan.

And yet, I see more people, both children and adults, smiling in Ankawa than I did in other countries with more material wealth and fewer everyday pressures and dangers. It is a community of belief, shepherded by clergy for thousands of years.

The trust in God is palpable here. Locations cited in the Bible are all around this region. Nineveh plains, the Tower of Babel, the Garden of Eden, the birthplace of Noah, and the city of Ur, birthplace of Abraham, are but a few of the most noted sacred places in Iraq. Sites of terrible massacres, battles and persecutions are also integral to this landscape. It is a land of blood and tears as well as of spirit and conviction.

This land contains rich natural resources which other nations have coveted for hundreds of years. In ancient times it was called Mesopotamia, translated as "the land between two rivers": the mighty Tigris and Euphrates waters. Babylon was a thriving, sophisticated city and known for such architectural feats as the Hanging Gardens of Babylon and its rule of laws, a basic system of courts, a system of mathematics and writing. The name Iraq is translated as "fertile" giving an indication of what this country contained for thousands of years.

By the time I arrived there in late 2017, because of the technologies of 21st century wars, including the use of depleted uranium bombs, poisonous gasses, chemical weapons, napalm and landmines, the once fertile lands of Iraq are contaminated. The waters are polluted with toxins from weapons, industrial runoff and dead bodies. Yet, the people still rely on agriculture and fishing for food. They raise sheep and goats on the sparse grasses growing over battlefields and between the ruins of war, or around the unfinished building developments halted by corruption or war.

Life in Ankawa continues in near normalcy after the worst of the siege of Daesh/ISIS seems to be over. Restaurants are open, street markets for meat, bread, fish, vegetables, and other foodstuffs and clothing abound.

Open market in Ankawa. Fish from the Tigris River, Iraq 2018.

In our neighborhood, once a week, a truck selling milk, cheese and clothing drives around slowly with music pumped out of a loudspeaker. This is "door to door shopping," Ankawa's version of "home delivery."

This is my first time working and living in Iraq, although Kurdistan considers itself a separate state, and Ankawa is its own separate sector different in most ways from nearby Erbil. It feels familiar to me in a Middle Eastern way.

I had treated Iraqi refugees in the clinic we started at the New Zealand School of Acupuncture and Traditional Chinese Medicine in Wellington, from 2004 to 2006.

One of my patients was the Iraqi poet Najat Al Abdullah, from Misan. She spoke of her homeland with graceful longing. She fled from the regime of Saddam Hussein and

Chickens for sale at
meat market in Erbil,
Iraq 2019.

eventually returned to Iraq. I also treated a half dozen Iraqi men from Basra who had suffered torture under Saddam's reign. They were all Muslim and most of the men were still true believers. They wanted to return to Iraq someday.

The vast majority of people in Ankawa were Christian, with a different experience of life in Iraq, and their own traditional culture.

Herding sheep in Ankawa, Kurdistan, Iraq in 2018.

The Catholic church placed all of us expat faculty women in a house with one other young American woman, who was teaching at the Catholic high school.

There were only two of us American women on the CUE faculty at the time I started. The other woman was originally from Kazakhstan and had both Tatar and Mongolian ancestry, a fact she reminded us of often. She spent her university years in Russia majoring in English. Eventually, she worked her way to a job at the American embassy where she met and married an American who sponsored her for graduate work in the USA.

She still had a heavy Russian accent and she enjoyed smoking and drinking alcohol. She was divorced and an outspoken atheist, and it surprised me she was hired at this Catholic university until I realized she had a "special relationship" with the Iraqi Chancellor. He had dual citizenship in New Zealand and left his wife and family there while he lived as if he were a single man in Ankawa. He spoke four languages fluently and was connected to a number of networks besides the Catholic community.

He kept breaking various terms in our contracts, pleading he couldn't recruit any other suitable faculty. We were all forced to work at least 12 hours over our original face-to-face contracts each week. We were also promised "single accommodation," not shared housing. He would stall and promise us it "will be ready soon" but none of us believed he would ever find us the promised housing. He would stall until the end of our contracts.

Colleagues from CUE and author at Greek Grill
in Ankawa, Iraq 2018

Still, I enjoyed teaching and valued my CUE colleagues from Mosul, Qaraqosh and other towns. They were brave survivors of the siege of Daesh/ISIS. They were earnest, hardworking, intelligent and resourceful. I learned from them. We discussed world events, their view on what will happen to Christians, pedagogy, theology, and ways to support our students, almost all of whom were survivors who grew up with war and the cruel sieges and persecution by Daesh/ISIS. As time went on, some told me the histories of their communities and families, and a few recounted what happened to them personally.

Many of my students had witnessed terrible atrocities committed against members of their own families and communities. I was told most had been raped. That was the "tax" (jizya) Daesh/ISIS would extract as the price for leaving. No one was spared— not children, not the elderly, not persons of any age or gender. They would have to surrender all their possessions, their bodies and dignity.

There was no end to the cruelty and torture Daesh/ISIS perpetrated on these people. Their crimes included putting children and men in cages and burning them alive, killing infants and forcing the family to cook and eat their own child or the rest of their family would be killed. Selling children into sex slavery, beating children and women, branding them, and killing people in front of their family members. Daesh/ISIS showed no mercy. They filmed their depraved actions, posting the videos and photos on jihadi sites on the darknet.

Yet, somehow the community's Christian faith sustained them. The bishop opened his largest churches in Ankawa to those fleeing for their lives. He let them sleep in tents on the lawn or on the church pews and gave food and shelter at the churches until the refugee camps could be erected nearby.

The Catholic University in Erbil was set back from the main road in Ankawa. Only dirt roads led up to the entrance from three sides. The guards in front carried weapons and searched anyone they did not know before letting them through. However, like many guardhouses these days, they had large screens to watch both the perimeter and television programs. Often the guards' heads were looking down at their phones instead of out to scan for possible threats.

There were open fields next to the main buildings, giving easy access to the first-floor classrooms and computer lab. There was a definite difference in attitude here toward security than in Afghanistan, where I had spent the previous three years. It was, to my mind, too casual. The power or prayer can only do so much to shield one from harm. The phrase, "God helps those who help themselves" came to mind as I surveyed the university.

Life in Ankawa was full of activity. There was a well-equipped gym which held classes for card holders. I bought a monthly card and took strengthening exercises classes taught by a former Peshmerga female soldier. She was focused and a hard task master. I loved it.

I also took Zumba from a Russian woman. She would turn up the volume on the music and count out the routines in three languages, Arabic, Russian and English. She wore yoga tights with wild animal patterns and encouraged all ages to join. Dance is also a way to "work out" and express trauma, grief and fear in a healthy, physical way. Her classes were always full.

There were churches which held Catholic mass in the original language of the bible, Aramaic. I loved hearing this language and the music of the "Our Father" prayer sung in Aramaic. Colleagues invited to me the smaller churches in which the priests spoke Assyrian. One church in Ankawa held services in English and the priests were from Chicago and Detroit. A few of them spoke Arabic and/ or Aramaic. Contract workers from the Philippines, India, Russia and England would come to Mar Elia, also known as Mar Yousif which hosted events to heal the community. I would alternate between that cathedral and the Chaldean Cathedral of Saint Joseph.

The Chaldean community provides a number of local humanitarian relief services in Ankawa. They have their own governing body and security.

Chaldean National Congress building,
Ankawa, Iraq. 2018

I often passed by their National Congress headquarters on the way to shop in Ankawa. I always wondered what it was like inside.

Fortunately, I was invited into one of the Catholic monasteries in Kurdistan. They created a sanctuary of

Outside of the Catholic monastery in Ankawa,
Iraq, 2018

peace, beauty and devotion. You could feel the reverence within the walls and surrounding the area. It seemed in a world apart from the hectic life of Ankawa and nearby Erbil. I enjoyed traveling between those two worlds of the secular and the sacred in this ancient land.

2018 was a time of more political upheaval in Iraq. The "free and fair elections" touted by other nations after the war in 2005 were nowhere in evidence by 2018. As a bit of context, I include an excerpt from an article I co-wrote with Adad Shmuel entitled "Iraq 2018 Elections Aftermath—A Critical Situation for Christian Minorities" published in Small Wars Journal in July 2018.

The May 2018 election results shocked Iraq. Officially, it was the lowest voter turnout recorded since the first freely held elections after the fall of Saddam Hussein in 2005. According to the Institute for Democracy and Electoral Assistance (IDEA) Iraq recorded a 79.63% voter turnout in 2005. The recorded voter turnout in 2018 was 44.85%.

For minorities and their candidates, the election results have been catastrophic. Christian minorities, including Chaldo-Assyrian people, who are the indigenous people of Iraq, face serious types of persecution from those in charge of the current government. Both the Kurdish Regional Government (KRG) and the central Iraqi government elected officials have not kept their campaign promises regarding protecting minority rights.

The current situation for Christian minorities is extremely precarious. Christian minorities are now potential pawns of powerful rival political parties and are seemingly not supported by any internal or international power players.

The tens of thousands of survivors,and internally displaced persons from the sieges by Daesh/ISIS, had no voice in the political system by 2018. They had no place to live, and most had to leave all their possessions and savings behind when they fled. Their properties were taken over by the Kurdish and Arab investors who exploited them after Mosul was 'liberated' from Daesh/ISIS.

Catholic and Christian charities and a few international NGOs came in to rebuild parts of Mosul, re-locate survivors and set up more camps in 2018. The Iraqi government pleaded "no available funds" to rebuild Kurdistan.

Iraq has never recovered from "Operation Iraqi Freedom" which cost tens of thousands of Iraqi lives, trillions of US dollars and thousands of American and coalition lives. The war's death toll rose to an estimated 176,000 to 189,000 and cost more than two trillion US dollars.

The blood price for "democracy and freedom" in Iraq continues to be steep. For over a decade "civil society" and "capacity building" programs paid for with American dollars have yielded few sustainable results.

Security remains a serious concern for most of the country and for all tribes, ethnicities, religions and political parties. After infusing billions of US dollars, thousands of trainers and training hours, materials, weapons and personnel; Iraq has not successfully been able to maintain security on its own, yet. One has to ask why? What are the intentions and what is the incentive for the US government and private military companies to provide 'back-up' and 'support' for the Iraqi military?

There are many who would argue (within Iraq and the Middle East and within the USA and UK) that the aim of foreign policy of the western countries involved and of Iraq's middle eastern neighbors, is to keep Iraq divided, feeble and dependent *while her largest most lucrative resource-oil-is siphoned off and/or used for leverage.*

Unlike citizens of the Gulf Arab states where the Gulf Cooperation Council (GCC) governments in the region share oil wealth with their citizens through a large and well-paid public sector and through very low prices for energy; Iraq's citizens do not receive any share of the wealth.

Most of Iraq's sectarian and ethnic leaders believe the US strategy in 2003 was indeed divisive.[2]

My senior students in my International Relations course argued persuasively that the history of Iraq and specifically of Kurdistan since the defeat of the Ottoman Empire in World War I, was one of broken treaties and promises by the British, Iranian, Turkish and US governments. The internal control exerted first by the monarchy, then by Saddam Hussein and now by the Iraqi government influenced by the outside powers, meant that Christians and other minorities, including the Yazidis, would continue to be squeezed, under-represented, discriminated against, and sacrificed. The outlook for them as Christian Iraqis was grim.

---

2    "Iraq-Time for a Different Approach" 01/27/2020-*Small Wars Journal*

Aftereffects felt by individuals and families after decades of war include post trauma, depression, survivor's guilt, abject grief and other serious mental health problems. They've seen the tearing apart of families and communities, the loss of important historic and religious centers, loss of personal property and businesses, loss of education for the next generation from years of no schooling, the absence of security and the destruction of infrastructure.

Kurdistan and Iraq are severely wounded. But they still hold the most precious natural resources coveted by powerful countries: light, sweet crude oil and natural gas. This gift of nature is also their curse. Millions have died in wars fought to control these "gifts."

At the start of the second semester in 2018, I was offered a short-term consulting contract with the Center for

Wall mural by an elementary school in Ankawa

Intercultural Education and Development (CIED), a joint program with Georgetown University and the US State Department. I had worked with them since 2008 in a number of countries. This project was to be in Israel as part of the efforts to prepare for the US embassy to be moved from Tel Aviv to Jerusalem. I had interviewed for this position months earlier.

CUE had three weeks off in March for the Newroz holiday in Kurdistan, and Spring break. I would have to ask for another week off since the work would take one month. It would also mean I would fly from Erbil through Baghdad to Jordan, and then on to Israel.

I consulted with the Dean who told me to talk to Bishop Warda. When I explained the purpose of my work in Israel. He agreed I could take more time off and gave me a letter to take with me if I had any problems getting out of or returning to Erbil. He advised me to only show my onward ticket to Amman, Jordan, if asked for my final destination. I thanked him for his support. I assured him I would return to finish the academic year and summer school.

With the uncertainty of Iraq visa requirements, it was best if the US State Department routed me back to the USA, and then onward to Erbil. That meant I could also see my daughter for a few days before returning to Kurdistan—a belated birthday treat for myself.

My teaching load was heavy after I'd taken over for another faculty member who got stuck outside of Iraq and couldn't return. I was teaching two sections of Introductory Economics, two Political Science courses, one International Relations course, one Information Literacy course and co-teaching English for Academic Purposes with one of my Iraqi colleagues.

My language class was full of students who were provisionally accepted to CUE pending their learning all four skills of English at an academic level. Reading, Speaking, Writing and Comprehending. These students were right out of high school and young survivors of years of the Daesh/ISIS scourge. They were motivated and resilient.

I had worked in a number of countries where there was or had been conflict and trauma, where having another language to express emotions and harrowing experiences for those people could potentially open and exorcise those sufferings. Secrecy would be easier for them if others in their family or community did not know English. They felt more comfortable confiding in another language. English was not associated with the trauma. They could detach themselves from the past by describing it as if it were not part of them. In this way, learning another language could be therapeutic.

As much as I could, I praised these students and encouraged them, and required them to speak in English as much as possible. Most of my students already spoke at least two languages, Aramaic and Arabic. Many also spoke Sorani Kurdish. They could read and write in at least two alphabets.

One afternoon at the end of February, the weather was mild so I had the windows open. We could hear animals near our building. There was a shepherd with his sheep and a couple of dogs barking. The dogs moved closer and continued barking as the lesson continued. I noticed one of my students, who was usually quite shy and attentive, was staring out the window. She started shaking and suddenly turned pale. She began mumbling in English. Then her voice grew louder.

"I hate them. I hate dogs. I hate them."

She became rigid and kept repeating the same statements. The rest of the class grew quiet. I walked over to the windows and quietly asked her as I closed them, "Why do you hate dogs? Why do you hate them?"

She was still very pale and stiff. I asked her to please help me finish closing the windows. When she turned to look at me, I could see a faraway look in her eyes. She was in another time. She was remembering.

"Did something happen with dogs to frighten you?" I said her name gently.

She started to come out of her trance-like state. She looked at me and spoke in English.

"One morning, when we lived in Mosul, when I was young, my parents told me not to open the front door. There were dogs barking outside. I wanted to know why they were barking. When my parents weren't looking, I opened the front door. Just outside I saw three dogs. They were eating part of a body. It was our neighbor. They were eating him. I couldn't scream or say anything. My father came and took me back inside. I hate dogs. I hate them."

"Oh, I'm so sorry. It must have been a terrible, horrible sight. A shock."

Some of the other students got up and helped close the windows. As they did, one started recounting an incident where he saw his relative shot because he was hiding outside when he, too, wasn't supposed to be out of his house.

Another student said he remembered when he saw Daesh/ISIS taking his father away with other men and he couldn't run to save him.

For the next hour, I let students continue to recount their memories. A sort of dark humor was shared, too. By the next break we were laughing at the horrors. We were all speaking in English. We commented that probably nowhere else would this be a subject for conversation we could all speak about in a language lesson.

When we came back to class for the last hour there was a sense of relief in the room. The girl who had spoken about her memory of the dogs was more relaxed. There was a greater sense of comradery among the students. I sensed there was a shift in our relationship as well.

These were courageous and vulnerable young people. They taught me more about the human spirit's ways to process trauma. I said a silent prayer of thanks to be among such exceptional young people.

I suggested we end by learning a dance from Texas. A line dance where we could practice our vocabulary for directions, and they could hear another type of accent. I would be the "caller." My students liked to dance; dance is another way to express emotion within form and to experience joy and pleasure in that expression. Line dancing allows an individual to dance with others without having to touch or hold them. Also, males and females did not have to join hands. I had shown them a short video of some champion line dances a few days before.

We went out to the courtyard. I went over the basic moves and instructions. We ended the day dancing together. One small step toward healing, I hoped.

Over the next weeks, I prepared for my work in Israel in addition to my duties with CUE. I planned my time after work in Israel to be in California with Sequoia before I had to return to Ankawa. My Iraqi colleagues were supportive and curious about Israel. I promised to take photos and describe my trip upon my return.

When I got to California, my daughter had planned to take me to Skydive Perris to do a tandem skydive for my 65th birthday. Sequoia was serious about skydiving as another of her extreme sports. I wasn't so keen, but I wanted to know what she found so appealing. I remembered her father telling me how he got airsick sometimes before jumping out of airplanes during his US Air Force Pararescue training. I took some ginger gum with me in case I got motion sickness.

The plane flight up didn't worry me, but my daughter jumped out backwards, by herself. She didn't warn me, and I couldn't see her falling fast into the atmosphere. My tandem partner jumped out as I was still scanning the skies for my daughter. It wasn't a scary experience so much as a concerning one for me. When we landed, Sequoia was waiting for me on the ground.

"Happy Birthday, Mum!"

She took a video of my first minute getting my bearings. My reaction was, "I'm glad I tried it. I don't ever want to do that again. I don't understand the attraction of this sport."

We spent the next day together in Santa Monica and then she took me to the airport. My mother's heart beat faster knowing Sequoia was jumping out of airplanes for sport. At least she wasn't climbing in high altitudes, I thought.

I felt relieved when we landed in Erbil. I knew the driver who picked me up. The weather was pleasant in April, and the airport seemed less tense than I remembered. However, the situation at our house was the opposite. The younger American woman had been fired from her teaching job at the high school. Rightfully so, since she was consistently late to work, got drunk on the weekends, and hardly prepared for classes. Not a positive role model in a conservative, Catholic school. She was going back to the States.

We were told we had to move to another house next to where the Chancellor lived in a different neighborhood. This time I would only live with the Kazakh woman. The other American decided to get her own apartment since she would not be continuing her contract after the summer. She had a better offer in Oman.

It was a hassle to move. Our new accommodation was not as convenient, clean or as comfortable. I decided I would accept an offer I received to be part of a new university to open in Baghdad for the next academic year. It would be the new American University of Iraq set in the former palace of Saddam Hussein. They offered single accommodation, all relocation costs, a higher salary and a reasonable teaching load. The projected start date would be at the end of September 2018.

My contract with CUE ended around the same time. I heard a credible rumor CUE would be cutting costs and only hiring local faculty or faculty through the clergy. International expats were too expensive. We required accommodation, coverage for international travel, and more benefits to stay. We helped them reopen in 2017–2018 and enhanced their reputation as a bilingual university. We served their purpose. We were also a security risk. It made sense to phase us out.

End of term exams for my senior students were the last passage before graduation. The Catholic church provided a few scholarships to associated Catholic universities in Italy, the USA and Australia. I hoped a few of my best students would have a chance to leave Iraq. The chances for gainful employment and higher education were greater in other countries. For some, it would be safer to live outside of Kurdistan.

Summer exams at CUE in Ankawa, Kurdistan. 2018.

The disadvantage was they would have to leave their families. Many families had already lost members to violence while others had to flee. The number of intact Christian families in Iraq was diminishing fast.

Summer school classes were a mix of CUE students and students from other universities. We had more Kurdish, Muslim students on campus. A few nuns were also given scholarships to attend my class. One of them gave me her rosary after she heard I would not be teaching at CUE after September. She had survived the siege of Mosul and would be transferred soon to the USA. She was an enthusiastic student. She was always cheerful in spite of what I heard she had endured. Her perseverance was an inspiration. I cherish this personal gift and keep it with me always.

Café in Ankawa, Kurdistan, Iraq 2018

One of the places in Ankawa we went to have coffee or a snack was a café I nicknamed "Make Coffee Not War" because of a poster they hung on one of their walls. People of all ages, walks of life and communities congregated there. It was also a rendezvous point for a number of groups, including a hiking group which would post their trail routes on Facebook.

Since the siege by Daesh/ISIS had disrupted education in nearby Mosul and the surrounding towns and villages for over three years, the Catholic community decided to open up summer schools. The classes I taught for the CUE summer session were full. Students from other universities, students who were to start CUE in the Fall semester, and senior high school students from the local parish Catholic school were eager to improve their academic English.

CUE was air conditioned; the internet worked most days, and students did not have a strict dress code. The courses were popular. Ankawa was a safe area for the most part.

Although there were still isolated incidents of violence including car bombings, shooting and kidnapping, the more horrific mass torture and killing of Christians had ceased after intervention by the Peshmerga Kurdish military units, units of the Iraqi army and its allies for this fight, including the United States.

My Assyrian colleagues warned that Daesh/ISIS was not completely vanquished. They would regroup and strike again. Many Daesh fighters fled across the border to Turkey. Some fled further north all the way to Afghanistan. Many were given safe passage to Iran.

Persecution and prejudice against Christians in Iraq continued even after Daesh/ISIS was declawed. There was an underlying tension in Kurdistan. The future was uncertain after the failure to secede in 2017, and the Iraq government reprisals, including closing down the Erbil airport for over six months.

By May, 2018 the airport was open to international flights. I planned to vacation outside of Iraq once I was certain I could fly out. There was someone I needed to find who had worked in Afghanistan.

Toward the end of the summer, I had an opportunity to attend a professional development workshop in Malta.

Malta was not far from Erbil, and I had two weeks' vacation left.

I thought it would also provide an opportunity to take care of some unfinished business from Afghanistan.

Described as a strategic jewel in the Mediterranean, Malta was historically a place where negotiations, exchanges, money laundering, international filming and the Knights of Malta were located. It is the smallest nation member of the European Union covering three islands. English is one of their official languages.

I bought a round trip ticket from Erbil to Valletta.

# CHAPTER NINE

# Daphne's Ghost

I had the opportunity to do some professional development in Malta, a predominantly Catholic country in the Mediterranean known for its history, its beauty, its mild climate and safe, peaceful environment. This would be a welcome change for a short time before I would start a new position in Baghdad helping to create the first American University of Iraq, housed in the former palace of Saddam Hussein—an ambitious enterprise supported by wealthy Iraqi and American businessmen.

It would also be a chance to chase up a lead from Kabul, on my own time. One of the men who had been 'fishing' for information on me and my teammate and friend Lisa Akbari in Kabul, had a British accent and gave me a phone number to contact him in 2017. He said he was from Valletta, Malta. I figured it wouldn't be hard to find him or someone who knew him or knew about him. It was considered a safe place to travel alone as a woman.

I decided to travel to this place I had never been to before.

I arranged to house-sit for a couple who lived near Middlesex University's Malta campus. Their apartment was walking distance to a sandy beach and clear, warm, turquoise water of the Mediterranean Sea.

As soon as my feet were on the ground, I felt a connection to this island. The views were breathtaking and the air was clean and refreshing. I heard Italian, English and Maltese, a new language to my ears. People walked with a relaxed pace and the architecture was a balm to my eyes and spirit.

Throughout the history of western civilization, Malta was the site of refuge, battles, negotiations and healing. In fact, they have discovered the first human inhabitants arrived to Malta in the year 5,900 B.C. The Maltese have an older civilization than Egypt or the ancient Britons. Their temples from the Phoenician era are the oldest free-standing structures over the three islands of Malta and have been designated as a World Heritage site by the United Nations (UNESCO).

Malta has served as a place for world leaders to meet from the time of Napoleon through the end of World War II. Various religious leaders have plotted and sought sanctuary there including Muslims and Christians. During World War I, the wounded from the Gallipoli campaign were tended to on this island. Malta built the Mtarfa Military hospital which treated hundreds of Allied wounded in World War II. It served as a supply base for the Allies because of its strategic location between Northern Africa and the Suez Canal.

As a military base and fortress for the Allies, Malta was attacked mercilessly by the Axis forces. Malta endured some of the fiercest, sustained battles from 1939-1945.

Most people think of Malta as the setting for significant meetings between world leaders, such as the Malta Conference in 1945, which included President Franklin D. Roosevelt, Winston Churchill, members of the USA/UK military, intelligence and diplomatic hierarchy, held before the Treaty of Yalta. There was also the Malta Summit, a meeting between then President George H.W. Bush and Mikhail Gorbachev in December 1989, at which an agreement toward a proclaimed "New World Order" was declared signaling the end of the Cold War.

Going further back in history, most people will also associate Malta with the Knights of Malta Hospitaller officially known as the Sovereign Military Order of Malta (SMOM) aka The Sovereign Military Hospitaller Order of Saint John of Jerusalem, of Rhodes and of Malta (Latin: Supremus Ordo Militaris Hospitalis Sancti Ioannis Hierosolymitani Rhodius et Melitensis). They are known to be a Catholic, religious, lay order (a bit of an oxymoron already) who serve people in need. Originally, the Knights Hospitaller formed out of a hospital established in Jerusalem to treat Christian pilgrims via papal edict in the seventh century.

About four hundred years later, in the early eleventh century, the hospital was destroyed, but the mission of the Knights of Malta remained.

In 1126, they adopted the Maltese Cross. Its eight points denote the eight obligations of the knights, namely "to live in truth, have faith, repent one's sins, give proof of humility, love justice, be merciful, be sincere and whole-hearted, and to endure persecution."

Today, the Knights of Malta have established bases in over 100 countries and supported efforts in health care, education, civil society, religious, political and military endeavors. They have their own passports, diplomatic immunity and a seat at the United Nations.

However, as the organization grew and attracted nobility, their tentacles extended into the dark side of human nature and enterprises. Soon those who lusted for power and control also became members. The Nazis and later biker gangs and criminal organizations adopted versions of the eight-pointed symbol.

Knights of Malta

The Knights of Malta are not independent. They are and have been for centuries, controlled by the Society of Jesus or Jesuits as most know them. They are not independent. The Superior General of the Society of

Jesus (SJ or Jesuits) is known as the "Black Pope". The role of the Jesuits in assassinations and their extreme oath of loyalty is hardly noted in history books.

The Jesuits also oversee/control the Freemasons, Opus Dei, and P2—known as Propaganda Due, another "dirty tricks" arm of the Catholic church. They hold significant leverage over the Bilderberg group, Knights of Columbus, the Council on Foreign Relations, and Club of Rome, and have reaches into many criminal groups including La Cosa Nostra (the Italian Mafia). The leader of all Jesuits has a martial title, Superior General, and is known as the "Black Pope." The current Pope Francis is a Jesuit.

As former Naval Intelligence officer Milton William Cooper wrote in his landmark book *Behold a Pale Horse,*

> The Knights of Malta is a world organization with its threads weaving through business, banking, politics, the CIA, other intelligence organizations, P2, religion, education, law, military, think tanks, foundations, the United States Information Agency, the United Nations, and numerous other organizations.

> The world head of the Knights of Malta is elected for a life term, with the approval of the Pope. The Knights of Malta have their own Constitution and are sworn to work toward the establishment of a New World Order with the Pope at its head. Knights of Malta members are also powerful members of the CFR (Council on Foreign Relations) and the Trilateral Commission.

Malta has a "cash for passports" program, meaning it's possible for anyone to attain one. Maltese passports have been used to cover for terrorists' travel. Malta has also been used as a safe haven for political refugees and criminals.

HSBC bank laundered money through their Malta branch for decades.

"HSBC Malta has been fined €82,000 by Malta's anti-money laundering unit, the Financial Intelligence Analysis Unit (FIAU), for breaching anti-money laundering provisions. The FIAU found that the bank failed to adequately document the reason behind a €2 million transaction by one of its customers. In another breach, HSBC's transaction monitoring system failed to flag various high-value transactions by one customer, which at times reached €800,000.

The FIAU said that although there were rules in place at the time, there was no enforcement or anybody monitoring the accounts." From an article in the *Times of Malta* December 2022.

No triggers, or any alerts on the transactions carried out by that particular customer, were put in place for the transaction monitoring system.

The FIAU said the bank also stated that other controls in place, did lead authorities to scrutinize the transactions in question. The unit however noted, that the previously established monetary thresholds to monitor large transactions passing through Malta *were not followed.*

The Knights of Malta headquarters is actually in Rome, Italy via Bocca di Leone (mouth of the Lion). It is considered a sovereign state even issuing their own stamps. They have branches in many countries but the largest branch is in the USA, with headquarters in New York city.

They do have Dames as well as Knights. Much of their symbolism concerns black and white patterns which is similar to the Masonic patterns seen inside, outside and on ceremonial garb.

Part of the reason I am including this background on Malta is to lead into the recent events on this island concerning *The Panama Papers scandal.*

Knights and Dames of Malta in Rome, Italy 2018

Published in 2016, the Panama Papers was the work of more than 350 reporters from 80 countries and was coordinated by the International Consortium of Investigative Journalists. *The Panama Papers* are being called "the Wikileaks of the mega-rich."

The Panama Papers investigation was based on 11.5 million documents (emails, bank statements, passport photos and more) from Mossack Fonseca, a little-known but powerful law firm based in Panama. The investigation was centered on nearly 40 years of data from the firm, which had 35 locations around the world. It was one of the top creators of shell companies, which are corporate structures that can be used to hide ownership of assets. The firm closed its doors in April 2018.

Maltese journalist Daphne Caruana Galizia was one of the most rigorous investigative journalists involved in the Panama Papers. Throughout her long career, she filed evidence for anti-corruption reports, traced global money laundering operations, exposed child trafficking and child sex rings routed through Malta involving world leaders, high profile financiers, entertainment industry players, internationally known sports players, celebrities, arms dealers, weapons dealers, medical industry players and politicians.

Daphne Galizia probed the suspicious crash on Malta's Luqua airport runway in October 2016. *The plane carried five French officials who were investigating child sex trafficking rings and drug smuggling.*

"The French defense ministry said the plane had been working on its behalf, carrying out 'reconnaissance missions in the Mediterranean.' The flight was part of a French customs surveillance operation which has been taking place for the past five months, with the aim of tracing routes of illicit trafficking of all sorts, including human and drug trafficking," (From an online article by i24 news international. October 24, 2016)

Daphne Galizia's investigations reached all the way to the top leaders of numerous countries including the USA. Her thorough, detailed research infuriated those who had worked diligently to hide their illegal deeds. She found documents linking shell companies and trusts laundering money for political and business power brokers in New Zealand, Panama, Argentina, the USA, Russia, the UAE, the UK, France, Ukraine, and over 150 other nations. 214,000 tax havens were exposed.

The Sherbank corporation,originally registered in Russia, had direct links with Hilary Clinton's campaign fund, the Clinton foundation and Tony Podesta. The documents displaying the money trails for these links are also included in *The Panama Papers*.

Over the three decades Daphne reported on national and international cases, she was beleaguered by over 40 libel suits, her house was burned down, three of her dogs were killed, and she received death threats targeting her and her family. Her husband, a lawyer, and her three sons were harassed. Although incidents were reported to the

Maltese journalist Daphne Caruana Galizia.
Photo in Times of Malta.

local police, the Maltese government ignored the escalating intimidation tactics and created a culture of impunity for anyone attacking journalists.

On the morning of October 16, 2017, Daphne Caruana Galizia was killed when a car bomb planted under the seat of her car exploded by remote detonation. She was driving near her home when it happened. Her youngest son found the parts of her body in a nearby field. Her assassination sent shockwaves around the world.

When I read about Daphne Caruana Galizia's work and her assassination in Malta, I was preparing to fly to Iraq for the first time. The story of her courage, her career, the horrors her family was put through, affected me deeply. She was a noble woman who suffered a great injustice. I continued to follow the reports from Malta about her.

As fate would have it, I was able to view and walk about the memorial created for her right in the center of Valletta, under a monument to the fallen Maltese during the Ottomans siege of 1565, sculpted by Antonio Sciortino.

It hadn't even been a year since her death by the time I stood and prayed at the spot where supporters placed fresh flowers, letters, notes and photos in remembrance.

Daphne Caruana Galizia's memorial in Valletta, Malta 2018.

Lisa Marie Akbari – Born in Alabama, USA, November 9, 1980. Fatally shot in Kabul, Afghanistan December 20, 2015. Photo from her Facebook page.

August was a time when tourists from Europe swarmed over Malta. I was just one of thousands who came to pay their respects.

After my short pilgrimage I looked for a quiet location to place my call to the number I was given in Kabul. This man had somehow seen my report that was on President Ghani's desk along with other reports concerning the education system in Afghanistan and corruption found with the misuse of USAID funds. Although our names were supposed to be scrubbed, he said my name was definitely on the report along with that of my good friend and teammate, Lisa Marie Akbari, who was assassinated in Kabul in December 2015, while we were working for Checchi and Company, on a large USAID project.

This man had called me on my new personal cell phone when I was working in Kabul in 2017. I could tell right away he was on a fishing expedition. He used the line,

"Haven't we met at...?" He spouted a few spots where expats used to meet in Kabul, but none were places I frequented. He was trying to 'place me' but I listened and only replied in the negative.

Then he said he knew where I was and wanted to meet me. I declined and asked how he got my phone number and what he wanted.

He was vague about how he knew my name and number but did say the name of a woman I knew. She was originally from South Africa and worked with a logistics company that contracted with the US Postal Service in support of the US Military. We were acquainted tangentially. She was known as a gossip. I wondered what she might have told him and why.

He added he had read our report from our USAID research project. He read a section I had written, which concerned me. How did he get hold of a copy of that report? I excused myself and said I would call him back. I never did. There was something spooky about this man and his supposed work in Afghanistan. I suspected he was a cut out.

A woman answered the phone in Malta. When I told her XXX had given me this phone number, she let out a torrent of invectives against him. Apparently, she was his third wife and he had left her in debt and split to South America, or so she thought. She had nothing good to say about him and no forwarding address. She sounded angry, bitter and asked me for my name.

"Sorry, I'd rather not say," I answered and then hung up.

It seemed I'd reached a dead end in finding this man in Malta. Unless she was covering for him. It was hard to know without actually seeing her. I decided I wouldn't pursue him further.

I redirected and phoned my old friend, a British man I knew from my performing arts years in New York City. He now lived in Gozo, one of the other islands making up the archipelago that was Malta, and knew the islands, having lived here for many years. After our time together in Circle-in-the-Square Professional Performing Arts School in New York City, he had returned to England and done quite well in the entertainment field over the next decades. It had been almost forty years since I'd seen him or any of his family in the UK. We had connected over social media. It is useful sometimes.

When he answered my call, I recognized his voice right away. He offered to come to where I was in Valletta and take me to a place he knew in the center for drinks. We set a time for later that evening. I was curious to see him again.

In the late afternoons I was free to wander down to the beach and dive in the warm, clear water. It was so refreshing to swim again and snorkel. The beach and swimming area wasn't crowded. A few families staked out their spots with umbrellas and towels. Children were speaking Maltese and Italian. I relished my time there knowing I only had two weeks away from Iraq. I found it was better not to stay away longer than three weeks or I got too complacent with being in a safe area. I needed to keep my edge.

When my friend arrived to pick me up, he looked very much the same as I remembered him, just greyer hair, a sun-tanned, wrinkled face, and the same teasing temperament. He drove capably through the narrow streets at night and parked on a hill. We walked down to the tourist and expat center of Valletta.

It was a lively and slightly wild scene of music, impromptu dancing and outdoor tables, different from the tamer, more residential, local area where I was staying. It wasn't a place you could talk to each other easily but there was plenty to see.

As we walked back up the hill after a few hours, we were able to speak more freely. He had been drinking and it loosened his tongue. I kept to my usual tonic water or orange juice. We spoke about our lives and how divergent they were from what we'd envisioned. He told me about his son, his parents, his brother—all of whom I had met on a visit to England years ago. He told me Malta was the best place for him to retire and of the film and television work he was able to find, as well as part time teaching. He was content with his life for the most part.

My life is often challenging to explain to someone who has never lived or worked outside of first-world, Western countries. He could imagine, but not relate. He could understand not just taking a job for the money but for the mission.

We reminisced about the shows we had done together and that he had seen when I performed at the Edinburgh Fringe Festival back in the 1980s. He had come up to watch, and that was the last time we had seen each other. We arranged to meet again before I left. He dropped me off around midnight, then returned to his home in Gozo.

I dreamt all night of being back on the stage in New York and of being mesmerized by the colored stage lights. It was intense dreaming. When I woke to the sound of the ocean and brilliant sunshine, I was cheered. That part of my life's work was finished. My world has enlarged and been enriched since my time in New York City. I had no desire to go back.

Although I was supposed to be on vacation, I kept receiving requests from my CUE colleagues and the dean. They knew I would be departing from Iraq a few weeks after I returned and wanted to squeeze the most from me before I left. I swam off my annoyance in the Mediterranean every day. For me, it is the best stress relief, swimming in the sea or the warm ocean.

The few new people I met in Malta were young and full of ideas. Malta hosted and encouraged digital nomads, even offering a special "digital nomad visa." Experimenters in the fields of ICT and gaming came to Malta to meet other like-minded entrepreneurs. They could bid for financing from wealthy players who had offices or remote workers on the island. It was a great place to network in person, in the numerous cafes and shared office space around the island. The climate was also a factor. It was never too hot nor too cold in Malta.

There was a beautifully restored Orthodox church about a kilometer from where I stayed. It had originally been carved from rock and had three levels. I went to mass there a few times. Each time the church was full of what looked like local parishioners. Most of them were well dressed for church. The services were in Latin and Maltese, a language I found to be musical.

My friend and I met once more before I was due to fly out of Malta. He invited me to visit his home and to meet his lady friend next time I came.

Once at the airport, I switched my mindset to be more situationally aware. Vigilant. Ready to re-enter Iraq. It would be as if I were arriving to another world, a world apart from the ease and beauty of Malta, still haunted by the ghost of Daphne Caruana Galizia.

# CHAPTER TEN

# The Druze

The "Holy Land" to millions of human beings on Earth, is the nation of Israel. While it is known as a nation of Jewish people, the landscape holds sacred sites for a number of religions including the ancient polytheistic religion of the Judeans, the Zoroastrians migrating from Persia (Iran), and the newer religions of Christianity, Islam, and Bahai.

One sect which is unique to the Levant area including Israel, are the Druze. They are categorized by outsiders as having roots in Islam. However, they call themselves "Muwahideen," translated as "declarers of oneness." Their religion is an integral part of their ethnic community which dates back more than one thousand years. Their theology is based on sacred texts concentrating on the role of the mind and truthfulness. They are considered followers of an Abrahamic religion although they believe in reincarnation.

Not much is known or revealed to outsiders. There are very few permitted marriages outside their ethno-religious community. They do not accept converts. Membership is based on birthright and ancestry. They are deliberately secretive and exclusive. They make up between 2-3% of the population of Israel. They serve in the Israeli Defense Force (IDF) and are known as some of the best scouts. They have their own military Druze infantry unit called "Herev" or "Sword Battalion".

The Druze speak Arabic and those living in Israel also speak Hebrew. The ones I worked with, in 2018, also spoke fluent English. When I was contacted about being part of a project in advance of moving the US embassy in Tel Aviv to Jerusalem, I didn't know much about the Druze except that they were great scouts. I had met a few before when I hitchhiked around Israel in my twenties. In the intervening years, during my trips and work in Israel, they were not present in the places I frequented.

However, shortly after arriving to Tel Aviv from Baghdad, in March 2018, I met my Pathways organization teammates at the US embassy. This was the subcontracting organization funded by the US State department Near East division. The project to train high school teachers and students from different demographics throughout Israel was part of a package of projects designed to ease the transition of the US embassy moving from Tel Aviv to Jerusalem in 2018.

We drove to our first school for training. It was a Druze school. Druze high schools were among the highest performing on Israel's standard exams. Contrary to the way they are often characterized, Druze women have respect, equal opportunities and important roles in Druze society. Education is valued. There we met a number of Druze teachers, both women and men. Their high school students mixed with high school Jewish students from the public school district.

Due to security reasons, the Pathways Negotiation workshops were held in the 'miklat', also known as the Merkhav Mugan or "protected space" or colloquially as the 'mamad'. It was in the basement, with reinforced concrete and no windows. Cell phones didn't work in this large room. Students and teachers were used to working in these spaces. In Israel all public buildings and most private homes and apartments had their own 'mamad'. Sound reverberates in these underground, bunker-like places. It is a challenging space to teach in.

It was my job to observe, report and make suggestions for improvements for each training and workshop. I was paired with one of the Druze teachers who was dressed entirely in black. She was young but had the eyes of someone much older.

During one of the breaks, when we were getting to know each other, she mentioned to me her nephew had just died. He was in high school and many of the students knew him. The funeral was a few days before. There was a lingering sorrow on her face as she spoke.

Then she talked about the Druze belief in reincarnation. This surprised me. She said this was one of many beliefs that set them apart from the Muslim community and caused Muslims to have antipathy toward the Druze.

"There is a deep joy we feel especially after a young person dies. He will come back again. He has just crossed the door of this life and will enter again. We mourn, but we also have faith that this soul will be reborn."

We would meet again during the month. I wanted to hear more about her beliefs, if she felt comfortable telling me. She had an inner grace about her.

When the day of workshops was finished, we shared a meal together and both groups of students sang songs out in the courtyard. A major aim of this project was to bring people from different sectors of Israeli society together in a collaborative way to learn negotiation techniques. As in most places, music, movement and good food were a way to develop rapport.

My Israeli teammates were from other countries originally: Australia, Canada and the USA. We spoke half English and half Hebrew together. I was the only female and older than my colleagues, who were all in their late twenties and early thirties, so I acted as a team lead and a sort of "auntie." We took public transportation and a rented car. I adjusted to their casual dress and easy teasing with each other. It was the most enjoyable short-term project I had been part of in a long time, and a welcome break from the tensions in Kurdistan.

Destination signs just outside Givat Haviva.

The next schools we would visit were further north to the Kibbutz Federation National Education center. The kibbutz name is Givat Haviva in Menashe. It was established in 1949, as a way to promote peace between the Jewish and Arab populations and is located next to the Arab city of Baqa al-Gharbiyye. They host dual language courses in Hebrew and Arabic, as well as an excellent English program. Givat Haviva serves as a research center and runs national and international teacher training programs. Pathways programs of negotiation were of interest to them, as they were to the neighboring Arab schools. This was a place we would work for the next few days.

We met more teachers from both Jewish and Muslim sect communities in this area. I was invited to visit the female section of the Arab high schools and sit in the lounge with the female teachers. My halting Arabic was enough

Front foyer of Al
Qaseemi High School.
March, 2018.

to communicate about basic observations and for all of us to laugh at. They were curious about my experience in other Arab countries and my views about the differences in systems. They were grateful they were in a country where education was valued and supported. They invited me to stay for dinner, which I did. Then with a full stomach, I returned to the rooms my teammates shared on the kibbutz.

This kibbutz was very upscale from the kibbutzim I had lived and worked on in my youth in Israel, (kibbutz Elot and kibbutz Sdot Yam). And from those I had visited in the last few years in the Golan heights. We spent the rest of our evening reviewing what we had seen in both centers and planning for the school events in Haifa, the Galilee and after, back to Tel Aviv for meetings and workshops before heading south.

What we discovered in the first weeks was that technology made our work more challenging. Students used their cellphones to screenshot our handouts, case studies and

Main building of Al Qaseemi High School
in Baqa al-Gharbiyye

quiz questions. They sent them to friends in other schools around Israel. Therefore, students already knew what to expect and had the answers before we arrived. Once we realized this, we had to change our approach and create new assessments for each school.

The teachers, with our guidance, worked out new strategies for teaching, compiled resource lists all schools could access, and worked through their differences peacefully. We made weekly progress.

Teenagers are some of the best troubleshooters. If you have patience, they can be refreshingly honest and often see loopholes in logic adults miss. They are open minded enough to think outside accepted societal paradigms. In my

Pathways teacher training workshops in progress
in Jerusalem, Israel 2018.

work, I found Israeli, Russian, Iraqi and Borneo students
to be the most resourceful and imaginative, as well as
hardworking. These Israeli high school students taught us
throughout our project. But sometimes their "creativity"
was frustrating. We had to continually adapt.

Our selected group of teachers adapted as well. They
came together to brainstorm curriculum using negotiation
education techniques for Israeli public, religious, Muslim,
private, Catholic and other Christian schools. All schools
in Israel are required to have Bible study, for example, no
matter if they are secular or based on other religions. It is
considered civic and cultural education. It is also designed
to teach a moral code.

Teachers from all sectors in Israel, US DOS PAO, and author in Jerusalem, March 2018

All Israeli youth, male and female, are required to serve time with the Israeli Defense Force (IDF). There are lessons in the high school curriculum designed to prepare students for military or national service. Only the religious Haredi sects are not required to serve. In this way, Israel is unique in the world.

My Druze colleague did not go with us down south. It had been a few years since I visited Beer Sheva, and lived in kibbutz Eilot near the city of Eilat. Developments spread over both areas. There were large, new universities, schools, infrastructure, tourist facilities and transport. With the Pathways team, I observed classes in high schools and spoke to teachers and students.

Our last area to cover were the 'disputed territories' and Muslim schools in that sector. There was a decidedly different atmosphere and reception to our team there. The dress code was strict for high school girls. Security was evident outside and inside the sector. A few teachers expressed their dissatisfaction with their situation and with the embassy move to Jerusalem. I listened. In the disputed territories and in the Arab sections of Jerusalem, the tensions were tangible.

We drove back to Tel Aviv for meetings and to help host an English language speech and debate contest for high school students. The US ambassador and various officials from the US embassy attended. A few of us had been invited to the Ambassador's residence beforehand. He told us this was his last posting before retirement. He enjoyed living in Tel Aviv. He wasn't keen to move to Jerusalem either.

English speech and debate winners at the Rabin Center, Israel 2018.

We had a few more workshops in Jerusalem before our final meeting with the US embassy personnel for an 'after action review'. My written report and recommendations were due two weeks after leaving Israel.

Before I left, I decided to spend my birthday with friends up north near the Golan heights. I had been to their place on the kibbutz a few years earlier. They had done more building and opened a small café since. One of the kibbutzniks offered to take me to the Syrian border to visit a few sites in the area I hadn't been to previously. He drove a jeep over the rough terrain and thought I'd be frightened or maybe impressed by his cowboy driving. But after being driven in Afghanistan, Ukraine and Iraq, his tour was tame.

Checkpoint at Syrian border to Al Quanitra
– Israeli side.

I took the bus back down to Tel Aviv where I had a few days to see some TCM doctor friends and swim in the Mediterranean Sea before flying to California to see my daughter, then flying back to Erbil.

A few of my new colleagues contacted me by phone and email. My Druze colleague sent me a list of resources for our new database and invited me to come see them the next time I was in Israel. They wished me safe travels and safety working back in Kurdistan.

I landed safely in Erbil in early April 2018. It was exam preparation time for all my students. They asked me questions about Israel. I was happy to answer.

Former Israeli soldiers from the Israeli Defense Force (IDF) had come over to Kurdistan to discreetly train Peshmerga units over the years. Israeli equipment had been donated since the early 2000s. Israelis supported the Kurdish referendum in Erbil in 2017, when neighboring countries did not. There are over 200,000 Kurds currently living in Israel.

Many people don't know there were thousands of Jewish Kurds. They are known as Mizrahi Jewish communities and have been subjected to the genocidal program of 'Arabization' since the 1930s in the Middle East. Most left Iraq in the 1970s, and then again in the 1990s, but it is estimated there are still about 700 Jewish Kurdish families in Northern Iraq. The Peshmerga accepted Kurds of all religions in their female and male units. They are fierce fighters and the most effective against Daesh/ISIS.

Kurdish areas in four neighboring countries.

While I was teaching in the summer session at CUE in Ankawa, I received news in July 2018, of a terrible attack on the Druze city of Suwayda in southern Syria. Villagers fought against Daesh/ISIS for three days and nights. The city of 170,000 was not protected by Syrian military or security forces. They didn't have enough weapons to resist an armed attack. Some said this lack of protection was a punishment by the Assad government for the Druze refusing or avoiding military service.

ISIS claimed responsibility for slaughtering at least 255 civilians, kidnapping young Druze children and women, taking them as hostages. Over two hundred Druze were injured. It was the first time the Druze were so deliberately targeted and brutally attacked by Daesh/ISIS. It was reported they started with suicide bombers and explosions, then went door to door killing whole families.

80 ISIS fighters were reportedly killed.

According to local officials, the Daesh/ISIS fighters came from the desert area bordering Iraq and Jordan. Thousands of Daesh fighters were scattered over Syria, Iraq, Turkey and Jordan. Their 'caliphate' in Mosul was destroyed, many of their members were in refugee camps and some in prison, but many had escaped. They were not entirely defeated.

Daesh/ISIS threatened to harm the hostages if "the Syrian regime did not halt its offensive against the Daesh/ISIS held Yarmouk Valley" near the Golan heights and Jordan.

Negotiations with such terrorists were futile. As with the Yazidi minority, no international support was provided. These communities were on their own.

The Druze may not have one leader that coordinates them in a number of countries, but they have a stalwart community. Thousands of Druze on the Israeli side, in the village of Buqata in the Golan Heights and from the Galilee, and other parts of Israel, gathered to discuss the attack that killed mostly women and children.

I expressed my condolences by email to my Druze colleagues in Israel, and my condemnation of these acts to my colleagues in Iraq. They knew all too well the torture tactics and ruthless, barbarous acts these hostages would probably be subjected to in their time in captivity with Daesh/ISIS.

Hostage bargaining began almost right away via the dark net. Photos were posted against the backdrop of Daesh/ISIS flags. The first of 30 hostages were displayed in August 2018.

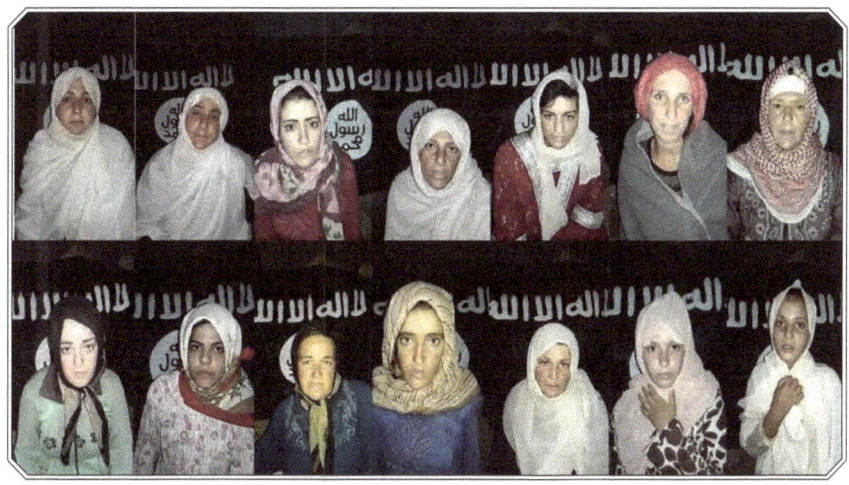

Hostage photos posted on the dark net sites in 2018

In October 2018, The Syrian Observatory for Human Rights released a statement that they "negotiated" with Daesh/ISIS for the release of 27 Druze prisoners in exchange for the release of 60 Daesh/ISIS prisoners and a payment of $27 million dollars. Daesh/ISIS would only release them "in waves." The first six were young women.

Druze families had been contacted after the attack for money to retrieve their family members. The world commercial, legacy press would not report on either the plight of the Druze or the hostages. *There was no formal condemnation by any of the western countries including the USA.*

A few more Druze were released in November 2018. This woman and her children were photographed upon their release by AL Arabiya news. You can see the distress and pain in their young faces.

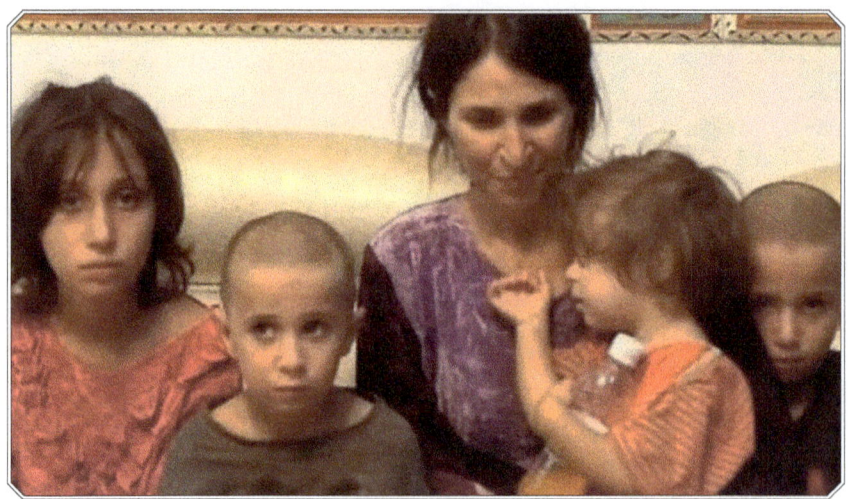

Part way through the hostage exchange agreement, Daesh/ISIS changed the terms of the deal with the Syrian government. Originally civilian hostages were to be exchanged for civilian prisoners. But after only releasing a dozen Druze hostages, Daesh demanded the terms be changed to include Daesh/ISIS fighters who were imprisoned.

Two Druze women had already died. One was shot and one died of illness while in captivity. The final deal included

ISIS fighters being swapped. The last of the Druze hostages were released on November 8, 2018.

Syria's foreign minister Walid al-Moallem declared that, at the time, "under the pretext of supporting Syrian Kurds, the U.S. has established bases in the North of Syria and a base in al-Tanf in the South, which are in reality used to reorganize ISIS terrorists to fight the Syrian Arab Army. What for? Because they want to prolong the Syrian crisis in Israel's interests".

Damascus also accused the US government of sending advisers to train and shelter Daesh/ISIS fighters they believed "had converted to moderate rebels", such as the Pentagon-backed Jaysh Maghawir al Thawra. The Syrian government requested that Washington either contribute to its anti-ISIS campaign in the Syrian Desert, or leave the area and let the Syrian army clean up the desert all the way to the Iraqi border.

The refusal of the USA to cooperate with the Syrians and the Russians in the battle against ISIS left a hole through which ISIS has been able to operate. The overland passage from ISIS territory in Iraq and Syria to Afghanistan ran through Iran. This route, and one through Turkey, with flights out to Afghanistan, gave Daesh/ISIS a way to flee and "fight another day."

And fight they do.

As we know in hindsight, Daesh/ISIS did regroup. Thousands of fighters from the offshoot group ISIS-K joined the Taliban in Afghanistan after years of in-fighting between the two terrorist factions. ISIS-K is the terror group's affiliate in Afghanistan.

In August 2021, the Taliban 'liberated' two large prisons, releasing their own members and other terrorist fighters from Parwan prison on the Bagram US military base and the Pul-e-Charkhi prison near Kabul. These prisons housed several hundred members of ISIS-K, as well as thousands of other prisoners. The Taliban took control of both facilities hours before taking over the capital of Kabul.

Eleven days later, on August 26, 2021, it was one of those prisoners who carried out the suicide bombing at Abbey Gate. ISIS-K took credit for the attack and named the suicide bomber as Abdul Rehman Al-Loghri.

Two US officials confirmed the identity of the attacker. *FirstPost,* an English-language news site based in India, reported that he had been released from the Bagram prison. His attack killed the 13 US service members and hundreds of Afghans.

The idea of the "new, reformed and kinder Taliban who negotiates in good faith" has proven to be a charade. Islamic terrorist groups used the time tried tactic to cheat and attack the "infidels" or non-believers. They utilized **taqiyya,** an Islamic tenant from the Hadith.

The Hadith supplements the Holy Qur'an in Islamic religious law. It is the second pillar after the Qur'an upon which every Muslim depends for guidance on how to live life and practice their faith.

The Hadith makes it clear that Muslims *are allowed to lie to unbelievers in order to defeat them or protect themselves.*

There is a historical "theology of rape of non-believers" that Islamic terrorist groups and individuals use as an excuse to commit heinous sexual criminal acts against children and adults of both sexes. They are taught to see these horrific abuses as "virtuous" for a jihadi fighter.

Islamic State courts are notarizing sale contracts for slaves—a how-to manual has even been published. 'Wholesalers' are buying women, numbering them like cattle, then advertising the sale of these girls to buyers. They can be bought and sold numerous times. Children as young as seven are considered 'prime merchandise'.

Slave auctions are still held in Turkey, Syria, Iraq, Pakistan, Saudi Arabia and other countries. Traders target minorities in these countries such as the Yezidis, Christians, Jews and the Druze. They are considered "Sabaya"—slaves. To them, they are property not people.

# CHAPTER ELEVEN

# Shala on HKIA

The fourth time I was sent to Kabul was to work on a Department of Defense (DOD) support contract with a multinational company. We went through Fort Bliss first in Texas, then took the long plane ride to Kuwait where we waited for transport to Bagram. At Bagram we had to wait again for transport to HKIA base adjacent to Hamid Karzai International airport.

Waiting meant spending time between the female transit barracks and the air transport waiting area. We didn't have much time to walk about the base because we could miss a transport. This was a much easier and, in most ways, a more secure way to navigate through Kabul than when I worked for smaller companies, or for the American University of Afghanistan.

It was coming on summer in 2016. The heat and dust made lugging my duffel bags a dirty, hot chore. Fortunately, there were a few others from the same company and we had met for orientation in Orlando, Florida weeks before. We spotted for each other while we were waiting and watched gear for each other. I was the only one who had lived outside the wire in Kabul or anywhere in Afghanistan. Working on military bases was a whole other world with its own rules and protocols.

I had visited HKIA a number of times from 2014-2016 for meetings on the base. But I 'd never lived and worked on base. I never had to wear a uniform except the "uniform" of being a woman under sharia law i.e., always wearing a hijab, long skirt, long sleeved blouses and long coats. The company uniform was simpler and practical. Cargo pants, boots, long sleeve shirt with a button-down collar.

When we arrived at HKIA the company project manager met us. He was brusque and seemed annoyed he was the one to show us around the base. There was only one other female in our newbie group. We were taken to the co-ed barracks. This was a NATO base. There were a number of different military units from different countries. In 2016-2017, the Turkish military ran the base. They took over from the British.

There was only one other female in our newbie group. We were taken to the co-ed barracks. There were two floors. I was told my room was with one of the interpreters on the first floor. The rest of the group were in rooms on the second floor. There were 150 rooms on each floor with ablution blocks/restrooms and showers in the center. One

Female transit barracks on Bagram base outside Kabul,
Afghanistan 2016

toilet and shower block were for females. The rest were for
males. Each room had two to three occupants. Most active
military were with their own countrymen or women.

Most companies had their contractors bunk together. I was
the exception. It didn't bother me at all that I would not
be living with someone I would be working with six days
a week, 10 hours a day. I was glad I would be with an
interpreter. Maybe I could learn more about the Afghan
languages and culture from her.

I knocked on the door but no one was there. It was just
before lunch. The Afghan maintenance man opened the

door and helped me with my duffel bags. I thanked him and closed the door.

It was an over-air conditioned, small room with bunk beds, two stand up closets, two desks, two chairs and a window that was mostly blocked by the air conditioner. The mattress was reasonably thick and fairly comfortable. The only problem was that the room was not divided equally and the bed I was to use already had sheets, a blanket and a soft toy on it as if it were being used. The desk on my side had papers and a photo on it. I was puzzled.

We were to meet the program manager again in thirty minutes. I unpacked quickly and was about to change my socks when I heard someone outside turning the lock. She opened the door and we were both startled.

"Hi, I'm Joanne. I was given this room by our company. I figured this must be my side of the room, right?"

A short, dark haired, brown eyed woman about my age, wearing a company/contractor uniform with badges around her neck, entered the room.

"There must be some mistake. This is my room." She stood firm.

"No, no mistake. Is there someone else in here besides you? If so, we can go to supply and see what happened with the barrack assignments."

"Hmmm...no." She responded slowly.

I suddenly realized she had placed things around both sides of the room to make it appear as if two women resided there.

"My name is Shala." She extended her hand. "Nice to meet you."

She had only a slight trace of an accent other than American standard.

"Sorry, Shala but we are rooming together. Shall I move the wardrobe so I can have half, and you can have half of the room?"

Shala gave me a hard look. I figured it was better to do this right away and let her know I would demand my due. We cased each other and sensed we both knew we were each the "warrior" type in our own ways...short as we were. Shala was a couple of inches shorter. We each had fire in our eyes.

"OK," she said finally. Together we pushed the wardrobes into position as a kind of partition to create some privacy on each half of our room.

"Thank you. I know it must have been better being here solo. How long have you been on this base?"

"This is my third year," she answered. "I've got go get lunch. I'll see you later."

"Me, too. I have to meet my program manager. See you after."

I left first and let Shala lock up. I didn't have a key. My program manager hadn't given me one yet.

After an afternoon of getting my ID badges, my assignment, schedule, and meeting some of the other training instructors, I went to get my uniform and my room key. The program manager told me to come to his room upstairs. There was an air of sleaze about this man. I saw him try to be very charming in his interactions with the other females on the team. They were all much younger, late twenties to early thirties. I had been hired by HR and his assistant. He had been on vacation during the interview process over skype. I could tell he was disappointed when he saw me and realized I was an "older woman". I was also the most qualified, but as I was to learn, that really didn't matter.

He was never in any branch of the military. He was a civilian from North Carolina and somehow got this job through his contacts. I could tell from the first hours; he delegated all his work. His sidekick was also never in the military but was eager to please and smiled all the time. He walked slightly behind his boss chirping, "Yes, sir," no matter what task he was given. He dutifully laughed when his boss made a joke.

The program manager asked me to sign some papers including insurance beneficiary designations. He asked me straight away if I was married and had children.

"I was married with two children, but my son and his father were killed in July 2013."

He came around to where I was and started to put his arm around my shoulders. "I'm so sorry. That must have been terrible."

"It was," I said, removing his arm. "But it's been almost three years and I prefer to keep busy working. My ex was a USAF PJ. I'm not the touchy-feely type, sir."

He thankfully moved away and continued giving me instructions for all the paperwork. He seemed to sulk a bit, but I let him. He gave me a package containing my uniform.

"We only have one in your size right now but we should get more in next week. You need to be in this uniform during all working hours."

"Got that, thank you. Could I please have my room key?"

"Oh yeah," he reached into his pocket. "Do you have a key chain?"

"Yes, sir, I do." I reached in my pocket and attached my new room key.

"Cool beans," he said and walked me to the door. "Can you find your way back to your room?"

"No problem. See you tomorrow morning then, sir."

I breathed easier once I was back on the first floor and could be alone for a time in my room. The room was near the outside door and quite a way from the shower/toilet block. I would need to time my walk there and back, to find the pace for my daily routine.

A contractor USAF mechanic lived across the hall from me, with a US Marine. He was friendly with another USAF contractor from my company and they both invited me to chow with them. I was grateful for their company and their sense of humor. They were also big, muscled men and it wouldn't hurt for my program manager to see I already had some male mates on base. I enjoyed my first buffet meal with them. We each trained the Afghan military in different sectors for the 'Warfighter Focus' programs. I had a feeling these would be my "brothers" for my time on HKIA.

Shala was already lying in bed, talking on the phone when I returned from the DFAC (dining facility). I smelled Afghan food and noticed a plastic bag with what looked like Styrofoam takeaway containers. I was curious. I waited until Shala finished her phone conversation in Dari, the official language of Afghanistan and her mother tongue.

"Hello again," I said. "Do you have a few minutes? I have a number of questions I think only you can answer."

We spoke for the next two hours. Shala told me about how things really worked on HKIA. She included details such as the best times to avoid crowds in the gyms and the DFAC, where to go when the sirens went off, which military sections to avoid, if I had a weapon and holster to make sure I didn't leave them on a hook in the shower block, how to put some laundry detergent in with your clothes before dropping them off at the laundry window because they often didn't use soap, just water.

Shala asked me about my family, my ancestry and a little about my training. She shared she was born and raised in Panjshir. Both her parents were educated and stressed the importance of education for their whole family. She and her sisters were given high school exchanges in the USA, in the days when Afghanistan was still a monarchy and ruled by a Shah. They returned to Afghanistan speaking, reading and writing fluent English. She was selected for a job at the US embassy in Kabul. There she met her ex-husband, a US Marine. They had three children together and they traveled with him to different parts of the world for his work. One of her daughters was a Marine. One was married to a Marine. Her son was still in college. She had been divorced for some time.

She had also worked with USAID. We compared stories about certain countries including Pakistan, and different times in the USA. We both relaxed a bit more with each other. Shala told me her ex-husband was Jewish and she had been blindsided when, after some turmoil, they divorced. At first, she was devastated but then she found work and rebuilt her life. Her faith in Islam sustained her. She cautioned that she rose early for prayers (salat). I spotted a prayer rug draped over the one chair on her side of the room.

Shala offered to get me "local, fresh food" that she had delivered almost every day. We took a short walk about the base and she pointed out the post office, some restaurants, the laundry drop off, the gyms and other barracks. I observed her nodding to a number of Afghan men and to other contractors as we walked along together. She seemed to know a lot of people on base.

When we returned to the barracks, Shala kept up a whispered commentary as we went by each room. "Ukrainians live here, Romanians are in this one, Macedonian women are in here, this is where two tall, handsome Marines stay, the other Afghan interpreters live on either side of us, US contractors live in most of the other rooms. The barracks across from us are mostly Australians and a few New Zealand military."

Between our barracks on HKIA base, Afghanistan.
Photo by Shala Hammond winter 2017

We both set about getting ready for our early mornings. I took my towel and dopp kit to the ablution block to have a shower. Men were returning from night shifts. Some openly stared at the newcomer—me—while others just trudged back to their racks (beds). The ablution block was empty. I had a long shower and mentally prepared for my first day of training.

After sunrise breakfast I got into my contractor uniform, boots, body armor and brought my ruck and helmet. I joined other members of our team of trainers at our pick-up spot behind the barracks. Some gave me a curt "good morning" before turning back to the road.

A few minutes later, the program manager and his assistant came by and said, "Good morning, team." He told me I would be in the main building known as "the pit" or "the circus." An Afghan-American man was the supervising trainer there. He would show me the set up and give me my roster and books. They would see me after the afternoon classes to find out how my first day went. Then he briefly introduced me and told the other members to "support" me in my first weeks. It was only then some of them smiled.

A van pulled up and we got in with our gear and went through one of the checkpoints manned by Triple Canopy company contractors, and out one of the exits to the other side. This was where the Afghan military stayed. No one said much during the ride.

When we reached the other side, we dropped off a couple of trainers at different buildings, then pulled up in front of a large, warehouse looking building with two US Army military guards. There was a military jeep and two civilian vehicles parked right up to the side of the building. I saw two portable toilets around the corner.

There was a makeshift bunker about 150 yards from the building. This looked like a cement culvert pipe cut in half and formed into a low-to-the-ground, tunnel-like structure. This was not like any other bunker I'd seen or been in over the course of my life in countries like Israel and Ukraine. When we stopped and got out of the van, I realized the driver was wearing the same uniform. He was also one of the trainers. Soon I found out we took turns driving the team to and from the barracks on HKIA to the other side each day. It was lucky I knew how to drive a stick shift and had experience with large vans since Marty always had a van we used for our family and for his work.

The guards nodded at us as we passed through the metal double doors into the "pit." I immediately understood why it was also nicknamed the circus. It was a cacophony in there. There were no walls, just flimsy partitions that you could shift in the space to create a classroom. These were only about 6 feet high. You could hear and see (if you were tall) into any other class.

There were eight of us trainers in the space. Each unit had a desk and computer for trainers, and tables and chairs for students. We were given a schedule for which lesson to teach on what day during the seven hours of face-to-face training with members of the Afghan military preparing them to go to the USA or the Czech Republic for specialized instruction in the various sectors of Aviation and Air Force training, in English. I was given the largest class of trainees—16 Afghan men squeezed into the cramped space.

The project manager's delegated supervisor in the circus was an Afghan-American man who spoke Dari and Pashto and reasonable English. He and his family had lived in Virginia for the last few years, where had been a pharmacy assistant at a CVS before becoming an interpreter and now a trainer. He knew what the students were saying, and he was the only interpreter to translate their comments back to us or the project manager.

He was earning a high salary with tax benefits by being out of the USA for eleven months at a time. He didn't want to lose his position. In essence, over time, I realized he ran the program. He was also a wheeler and dealer who had his prejudice toward fellow Pashtuns, and who ran side businesses (bribes for grades) for extra cash and influence. A line from Shakespeare's *Hamlet* came to mind after watching him over the next few months: "That one may smile and smile and still be a villain." He smiled constantly.

Shala was extremely busy at all hours of the day and nights. She was a CAT III interpreter holding a Top-Secret Security clearance. She would be called by high-ranking US military and politicians offices when they would visit HKIA. In addition, she would be zipping around in her golf cart-like vehicle checking up on her Afghan family (yes, she had nephews and cousins working on base) and friends. She was like their mother or auntie and would help them solve problems or give them advice and comfort.

She had been on HKIA a long time for a contractor, long enough to see the difference between when the British were in charge and now the Turkish military. She could discern which Afghan interpreters knew their languages and which did not. Which came from which part of Afghanistan, and which ones came from upstanding families or not. Most Afghans hired by 2016, especially the young males, were in the "not good" category. Contracting companies didn't really vet or know how to vet these people, they just wanted to fill slots and get the US taxpayer money for the human resources they provided.

Shala Hammond, on the right,
in Afghanistan with a FET US unit, 2013

We got to know each other quite well. After all, we could hear each other's Skype and phone conversations. We could hear a page turn, we lived so close, and we knew each other's schedules and saw each other's visitors.

Fortunately, we were a lot alike in important ways. For example, neither of us could tolerate what we labeled 'Crossovers'. A crossover was anyone from the US who fraternized and had sex with Afghan trainees or staff, or even with other countries' military such as the Turkish or Ukrainians. We thought they should have been fired and sent home. They were security risks.

We could hear through the walls that some of my company team females were 'fraternizing' with the young male Afghan interpreters in their room. Two of my female company colleagues, both in their early thirties, had laughs which were unmistakable. Another woman trainer from our company was having an affair with one of her high-ranking Afghan military students. He was married with children, and she was divorced. They even went on vacation to India together. He was "specially selected" to receive training in the USA. She came to our room one night because she thought I had seen her with this Colonel and photographed them. She was wrong; I hadn't. Shala watched her speaking with me. After she left, Shala confirmed what I suspected.

"Oh, she's definitely involved. I'll find out more from my contacts...quietly."

We did have fun sometimes watching various women go in and out of rooms in our corridor late at night. I would work out about 11 pm to avoid the crowds in the large tent gym. Shala would awake at 4:00 for prayer. One of the "tall, handsome Marines" that lived in our corridor had lots of activity going on in his room. Sometimes he would stand at the door naked to the waist, waiting for the next woman to have her turn. If one rotated out, it seemed that room always had another "tall, handsome Marine" to replace him in the barracks.

While I'm on the subject, I will give my considered opinion about accommodation on military bases after spending time on co-ed and single-sex barracks on bases like HKIA, Brize Norton (UK), NKC (Kabul), Fort Bliss (USA), Bagram (Afghanistan), Kuwait, and others.

Co-ed barracks do not add, but rather detract from "Mission Readiness". There are too many opportunities for other-than-professional encounters between males and females in almost any and every sheltered space on base, or outside the purview of surveillance cameras outside.

There is added tension and stress for both genders having to be with each other in corridors, shower blocks and during air raids at all hours of the day and usually night. There is further pressure because there is a hugely unequal ratio of men to women—probably at least 25 males to one female. On some FOBs (Forward Operating Bases) it could be twice that. Sexual tension and competition for female attention rises in those circumstances.

During my year on HKIA, on our floor, there was a double murder by two drunk Romanian soldiers who stabbed each other to death over a female. Oh yes, you could find almost any drug and most types of alcohol for the right price on HKIA. There was no x-ray or imaging machine to scan packages coming into the base through the post. And if you had a military badge, you could easily sneak in whatever you like. Your vehicle was searched if you came in by road, and you had to leave your weapons if you came in by air transport, but your person, your clothes, your body, were not searched if you had a badge.

There were a few restaurants on base which had supplies delivered. There was a Turkish restaurant Shala and I went a few times on our hours off. They had a large poster on the side of one corrugated iron wall. It gave the illusion of looking out at a beach.

Shala and author at a Turkish restaurant HKIA, Afghanistan, 2016.

HKIA contained a pizza place, a US run restaurant open seven days a week, and a coffee café. HKIA also had a beauty salon and a barber shop on base with beautiful, young women from Bishkek, Kyrgyzstan serving there. Ganci (the unofficial name for the US Military transit center base, Manas) also served as a staging and transport hub for the US and allied forces' invasion of Afghanistan. It was established in Kyrgyzstan in 2001. There was an exchange of service personnel between Afghanistan and Kyrgyzstan.

Larger bases such as Kandahar (KAF) and Bagram (BAF) had even more western type places to eat and recreate. Locals were required to service, supply and dispose of waste from these establishments. Therein was a wide opening for "trade" and smuggling. Even the base laundry was outsourced to Afghans—literally another way to "launder" money, goods and people. I wondered when I saw young women and girls from Colombia and Morocco on base, or at expat hosted parties and events in Kabul and Mazar. Who or what organization brought them into a war zone? I actually spoke to some girls (and they were evidently girls and not women) from Morocco. We spoke in French. The Colombian women were speaking Spanish, and some had visible tattoos. There was also a Chinese connection with Chinese women working in restaurants and as masseuses.

HKIA allowed local business "souvenir shops" selling jewelry, clothing, handicrafts, antiques, art, and carpets. Entertainment included a section of the base lounge for video games, watching sports and movie screenings. One night a week, they had karaoke and talent contests. If you only stayed on base, aside from the RPG's coming over a few times a week, you might not realize a war was going on. It was two different worlds side by side.

I kept in contact with some of my American University of Afghanistan (AUA) colleagues, both Afghan and American. I worked there in 2014 and 2015, and a few of my US Army Human Terrain Systems (HTS) program classmates were also working on HKIA and other bases around Kabul. I was often invited off base to some of their gatherings and to give acupuncture treatments. Technically, we weren't supposed to leave base except if with my boss. He had a side business going at the "Green Village" in Kabul. Other than his assistant, he would never take any of us outside the base.

After Shala and I got to know each other better and she learned I had my Traditional Chinese Medicine herbs, tools and acupuncture needles with me, she asked about treatment for her bunions.

"All those years of wearing high heels catches up with you, doesn't it?" she remarked one evening.

"Can I see?" I asked her. "Oh, they're not that bad. I could treat them if you like. Have you ever had acupuncture before?"

"No, but I'll try anything."

I treated her that night and the rest of the week. I had some herbal ointments I shared. She was to put them on under her socks and boots. After a few treatments she noticed a difference and her pains eased.

"Can you treat insomnia? Sometimes, I might be laying down over here, but I'm not asleep. I worry about my children, about my family, too much I think."

Shala didn't realize it, and I didn't want to embarrass her, but she also snored loudly. I was cheered that I could help her with both health problems. Since I was a light sleeper, it would help me get more rest as well.

Over the next weeks, word spread. I teased that Shala had become my "agent". First some of her Afghan family members, then some of her teammates came to our room. I would hear a knock on the door and a male voice saying in a low voice, "Shala sent me..."

I treated contractors in a number of sectors. I told Shala to please not tell anyone else. I needed downtime. I never took money for treatments as that was against my contract, but I did take goods. My favorite for trade was cans of Perrier water. The water in bottles on base was filled with chlorine. You couldn't drink the water from the taps. I had a sweet tooth for good dark chocolate, too. Pretty soon my stash of 'goods' increased.

My friends on base and in our barracks asked me why these men were coming to our room. When I explained about the acupuncture treatments, they soon approached me about it, too. A few times some of them would "collapse" due to back, knee or stomach problems. I ordered in more TCM herbs. I gave out Po Chai pills regularly. Many got sick from the DFAC food at first. Po Chai is a traditional Chinese medicine that clears food poisoning, hangovers, nausea and "the runs," among its other properties.

If my patients were American, it was no problem to treat them in their room, but for Afghans or people Shala didn't know, it was better if I treated them in the clinic. I knew the USAF doctor deployed there. We were in an Aikido class on base together. I had treated him and another USAF active duty for sprained ankles. I spoke to him about working together on some of these contractors. He agreed since he wanted to learn more about Chinese medicine. He only knew dry needling techniques. The clinic was usually quiet at night. We could use two examining rooms for treatments.

Shala frequently went off base. As I was to learn over the first months, many were able to go off base on Thursday night and return Friday night or early Saturday morning. We created a signal in our room so that when she or I came in, we would know if the other was "out". It worked well. If either of our bosses looked for us, or sent someone to summon us, we would text each other.

In August 2016, I received two urgent phone calls—one from a colleague at AUA in Kabul, and the other from an HTS colleague on base. Two faculty from AUA had been kidnapped. They were snatched from one of the transport vans on their way home with a driver at night. The Taliban claimed responsibility. I had been transported in those vans and knew their system, which was not secure. While they changed the time and transport routes weekly, it was easy to take a photo of the schedule board at the university security office and circulate it. I knew the head of security at AUA. I knew, too, the drivers never carried weapons. The expat faculty were easy targets.

One of the faculty was American, Kevin King, and the other had just arrived from Australia, Timothy Weeks. I was asked if I could help in any way with some of my contacts. The hostage rescue team (HRT) took down the numbers I knew including Kevin's. I made some phone calls.

Photo of American University of Afghanistan van after Kevin King and Timothy Weeks were kidnapped in August, 2016. Photo Tolo News.

HRT were able to find where they were being held but there must have been a 'leak'. By the time the team reached the location, the Taliban had taken them further north. It was evident they had been there and left only a short time before the HRT arrived.

Earlier in the year an Australian woman, Kerry Jane Wilson, who worked in a program helping Afghan women, had been kidnapped in Jalalabad. The search for her was ongoing. I knew of her from years past in Afghanistan, but never met her. She had been working in Afghanistan for about 20 years. I was asked if there might be any possible information about her as well.

I was partial to helping Aussies as well as Americans. We had lived in Australia for five years and my son was born in rural Macksville, Australia. I still had extended family there. They were Aboriginal from the Gumbaynggirr tribe. I contacted my closest 'family' there for their special type of "help" by bush telegraph and of course, prayers.

Soon after, somehow Kerry Jane Wilson was found and released by the Afghan army National Directorate of Security. She was flown straight back to Australia where I understand she now works for Hostage International. Kerry Jane had been kidnapped by criminal networks. She said she was not assaulted or harmed during her captivity. She was very fortunate. The Taliban had kidnapped hundreds over the years 2015-2016. They killed a number of their hostages or others as collateral damage during the kidnapping. They particularly targeted those working in humanitarian aid for women and children.

Eventually, three years later in 2019, both Kevin King and Terry Weeks from the American University of Afghanistan were released by the Taliban after intense negotiations with the United States government. After at least three rescue attempts failed because the prisoners were constantly being moved, they were exchanged for three high level Taliban prisoners held by the Americans.

My work training the Afghan military in Aviation English was routine for the most part, except my boss was often on my case. Incredibly, he hired a Russian/American woman with a heavy accent, who was probably 50 pounds overweight, but she was a blondie. She was also extremely aggressive. She was put in the "pit" with us. She didn't know I had lived and worked in Russia, in Siberia in 2011-2012. I knew a number of Russian swear words. She was calling most of the women "suka" (bitch) under her breath. She had a very loud voice when teaching and she was constantly coming into my space to 'borrow' my materials, student chairs and tables. When I went to retrieve them, she would shout at me. She refused to talk reasonably and at one point threw a chair at me.

The US Army guards came over to find out what the problem was. It was ridiculous we should be having these types of petty altercations in a conflict zone, but we did. She called our boss, who loathed coming over to where we trained. When he arrived and heard our sides of the story, his response was to give me restroom clean up duty, and to move her to another location. This is what she wanted from the beginning. She would be by herself with only two or three students. But at least she was gone from our "pit".

However, the boss wrote me up and I had to deal with HR from our company. I knew he would probably not recommend me for the pay raise most people received after the first six months, and I was right. At least, Shala and I could speak about issues we had with our companies and work. We didn't work together but we could commiserate. We also liked listening to podcasts when we had time at night.

In the Fall of 2016, better WIFI was installed on base and in the barracks. We listened to Jocko Willink's podcast on discipline and leadership. It would turn out to be very helpful in my next job. We could stream somewhat, but that had follow-on consequences which affected the entire base.

As Shala noted, before there was WIFI in the barracks, people played cards, or sat and talked with each other, and generally socialized more after work. You got to know people from other countries, especially the Brits and Aussies since we all spoke English. You had to go outside the barracks to find a cell phone signal, too. You could see people at all hours outside walking around speaking in their own languages on their phones, and a strange sort of comradery evolved.

However, after the internet connections improved, within a few weeks people would stay in their rooms watching

TV shows and movies, playing video games and skyping more. External hard drives and flash drives supplied the forbidden porn. Fewer people spoke to each other and everyone submerged themselves in virtual worlds. Situational awareness was affected. Some people had their headphones or earbuds in when the siren sounded. They couldn't hear the sultry, female, British voice warning over the loudspeakers, "Incoming, Incoming...take shelter, take shelter."

It was coming up on my first break where I could leave Afghanistan for two weeks. My daughter was going to Nepal, and we decided to meet in Kathmandu, then fly to the Makalu region and hike in Num. She had met a sherpa who said they wanted to build a school there for the sherpa children up in the mountains. Sequoia wanted to raise money to help his effort. She had a friend, Chris, who was a full-time police officer in Nevada and a filmmaker and photographer in his spare time. He would be with her and film us on our venture with Tashi Sherpa. It would be my first time in Nepal. I was happily planning to be with Sequoia for my R&R, making new memories in a new country.

Upon my return from Nepal, winter was tough in Kabul. This was my third winter in Afghanistan and the first anniversary of my good friend and teammate, Lisa Akbari's assassination in Kabul. Shala came in from the snow one evening very upset.

"Oh, this poor boy. He has no family here and something terrible is happening to him. One whole side of his face has dropped and won't move. He can't close his eyes, they seem stuck. He can hardly eat and he can't smile. The imam told him, 'It's God's will and there is nothing more to do.' Do you think you could help him?"

"Possibly, Shala. It sounds like he has Bell's palsy. It can be brought about suddenly, especially in cold weather. Where is he?"

Author in winter on HKIA 2016.
Photo by Shala Hammond

"On the other side. I could come pick you up at lunch time and we can stay over there while you treat him in a hanger. Then I could take you back. I'll bring some food and tea. What do you say?"

"Maybe I could try, but we can't guarantee him this will work for him. It will take a few treatments at least."

"Of course. Yes, oh thank you. I'll pick you up tomorrow. You can give me your medical kit so your boss won't know. I'll bring it in my vehicle."

"Ok, Shala but just us three while I treat him. You can interpret. I need to refresh my knowledge about these conditions. I'm a bit nervous about treating a young military Afghan male by myself given the cultural taboos."

"Don't worry. At lunchtime no one should be in the office where you can treat him. He knows he will probably be told he has to leave his training and he's desperate. It's worth a try, Jo...right?"

The next day at lunch I told my colleagues I wasn't going to lunch. Shala pulled up and nodded to the Afghan/ American man in charge. He nodded back. Shala drove me to an office in the back of one of the hangers. She opened the door and I saw my patient. He was very young, and his face was distorted.

Shala interpreted as I asked him some diagnostic questions. He kept fiddling with a string with a piece of paper with writing on it which was around his neck like a necklace. I asked him to relax, sit back and to breathe deeply while I inserted the needles. He didn't flinch. I explained it would take about 30 minutes for the needles to do their work and then we would see what else needed to be done.

After about 15 minutes Shala and I observed his eyelids being able to close and his mouth relaxing. After 30 minutes his face was much less "frozen" and he could open and close his eyes.

As I was taking the needles out, he spoke to Shala and said he already felt his face more, and he could go to sleep now that his eyelids worked. He thanked me profusely.

I explained, through Shala, that he would need a few more treatments to be certain all his facial muscles were released and the palsy/frozen condition would not return. He agreed.

He stood up and tore the string necklace from around his neck and threw it in the trash can. He felt his face with his hands and kept opening and closing his eyes. He tried a partial smile, but I still needed to do more treatments to release those muscles.

"I will come back to treat you every day at this time for the rest of the week, alright?" He nodded affirmatively.

I repacked my medical kit and handed it back to Shala. We were both happy this treatment seemed to be effective.

Shala told me after we climbed into her vehicle that the reason he tore off his necklace was that it held a prayer from his imam. The same imam that told him there was nothing to be done about his condition and he would just have to accept it.

"You have just literally opened his eyes to another way of thinking in the world. You have also given him hope."

"Well, I'm going to read up a bit more on palsy cases tonight. There might be some other points I could try on him tomorrow."

Shala took out some local Afghan food and shared it with me. It was tasty. I smelled a little like saffron and lamb when she dropped me back at the pit.

The rest of the week I made an excuse not to go in the van for lunch and instead went with Shala to treat my patient. Each day he improved more. By the third treatment, some of the Afghan officers came in to watch. It made me a little nervous but my hand held steady and Shala assured me I was doing a fine service by showing this type of treatment and medicine could work. I prayed I could further help this young man and I wouldn't get in any trouble.

Shala and I exchanged more of our personal histories, our dreams for our children, ourselves and our country, during the times we were together in our room. Shala taught me more Dari words and phrases and introduced me to more nuances of Afghan culture and traditions. As she observed once, "In some ways when I'm in Afghanistan I feel more American, but when I'm back in America, I feel more Afghani. I am between the two countries I love. I am between worlds."

I knew what she meant. I had the same feeling whenever I visited or lived and worked in Italy, as I had in 2013 and 2015 and earlier in my life.

Shala and I both worked through the Christmas and New Year holidays. She had time off in February to see her family. I was already being approached about other jobs with more responsibility in a different sector and on a different base in Afghanistan. It was clear to me I didn't want to stay with this boss or company.

Author treating AF military patient on HKIA.
Photo by Shala Hammond

There was one particular incident that reinforced that I was not with a team that would back me up in any way should danger hit. I think in poetry and even in dance during times of high stress, and the following is a poem I wrote about that particular incident that happened while we were teaching. I titled it, "What To Do In A Bunker" by Jo Patti.

## What To Do In A Bunker*

A familiar, sensual, liquid voice announced
Surface to air missiles
Incoming....take shelter...take shelter
Thud...the building shuddered...we looked

To the ceiling, to the door...continued training
The sultry female British voice declared another
Incoming...take shelter...take shelter
Whistling then crack, pounding, smash
This one was too close
Afghan military students
Spring up, run to their own places to hide
Leaving us to the mercy of our own God
Grabbed my helmet, backpack, followed
The designated leader who had no idea
Where we were supposed to go
Our American guards were new
They didn't know either but they
Had the guns and the comms
Take shelter...incoming...incoming
We quick marched outside to the sound
Of shattering glass, concrete blasting open

Crouching down in a large cement pipe
A culvert we call a bunker
It is slimy, cold, open at both ends
Half the team are without helmets
Forgot their gear - remembered their cigarettes
The girl beside me takes out her spy phone
She cusses as she scrolls furiously
I call the project manager on my flip phone
He's on the NATO base taking a nap
"Stay put for a few hours" He shouts
From the other side
He's not in harm's way
Incoming...incoming...take...

The ground shakes beneath us
Our American guards scout another location
No joy
there is no other bunker
We hunker down to the sound
Continuing "Incoming...incoming
Twenty minutes, thirty minutes
The ordinance is relentless
What's the plan
How long do we stay she's shaking
She can't stop asking questions

There are no answers
The guards fall in with us
We who are leaderless
This girl is anxious, restless
She's squirming, scrolling, whimpering
Incoming...incoming...take shelter...take shelter
I whisper to her... "What are you doing?"
"I'm searching google for what to do" she explains
"What are we supposed to do in a bunker?"
She is panicking - rocking back and forth
"I can't get a signal. I don't know what to do."

The sentry soldier guards hear us
They state their instructions clearly
"Shut the fuck up and wait."
That's what you do in a bunker.[3]

---

3   This poem is published in the collection "CLASH-Poems from
    Conflict Zones" by Jo Patti. Available in print, Kindle and on
    audio with me reading.

Shala was due to be back on base, but en route through Europe, she received harrowing news. Her ex-husband, the father of her children, USMC Richard "Gene" Hammond, had been murdered. He was shot to death in his own car while on the way to work in Denver, Colorado, on February 14. He usually left for work between 3:30 and 4:00 am since he coordinated school bus transport for the public school district. There were no leads and no suspects. Shala took the next flight back to Colorado.

When Shala returned to HKIA, she recounted the facts she knew and told me about the funeral service. The one positive thing to come out of the tragedy was getting to see relatives from both sides of the family she hadn't seen in years. They were comforting and gracious to her. Her family put up a cash reward for anyone with information leading to the conviction of Gene's murderer.

Shala was understandably completely distraught. I gave her acupuncture treatments and Bach Flower rescue remedy to get her through the next weeks. She wept copiously at night. She kept apologizing, but I reassured her it didn't bother me. I was from an emotional Italian family, and I had already been through a sudden death tragedy in my own family.

"Cry all you need and want to, Shala. It won't disturb me. I promise."

Shala had to keep it together since she was the interpreter for, among other politicians, Senator John McCain. He had already made a visit to Kabul for his July 4th photo op and meetings. Now, he was coming over again.

Shala was busier than ever, which in some ways helped her to face each new morning.

I knew the feeling of such deep loss, especially of an ex-husband. Shala never really resolved issues with hers. There are no "do overs" in such life situations. We spoke about the fact that neither of us subscribed to a "no regrets" philosophy. We had regrets about some of our decisions. We had to navigate the rest of our life with the painful knowledge we might have done better for our children. But we couldn't at the time, nor could we turn back time.

Shala in younger days in Afghanistan.

Spring crept onto base. The mosque the Turks and the Afghans demanded was almost finished. The chaos that followed the coup against Turkish President Erdogan in July 2016 spilled over to our base. Two Turkish officers apparently shot themselves rather than return to prison in Turkey. One General was arrested on HKIA, and flown back to Turkey. Erdogan had any he considered "traitors" arrested, jailed, tortured and many were executed. The Turkish barracks were on the other side of our barracks. The Turkish military had their contract renewed to run the base in 2017-2018.

Training class 2016–2017, outside HKIA, Afghanistan.
Author in center.

I continued with more training classes, all the while knowing that as soon as I had a definite contract with another company, on another base, I would give my notice. Soon my prayers were answered. A former HTS team leader had left his Team Lead position at VTED NKC. I would be his replacement as an Acting Team Lead, but I would need to wait and return to the USA to go through CRC (Conus Replacement Center) for pre-deployment checks at Fort Bliss. Back to Texas I went—again.

My daughter had written a book about her trip to look for the remains of our family on K2 in Pakistan. She titled it *Journey of Heart*. It was doing well in the USA, and Sequoia wanted to do a book tour in New Zealand, her place of birth and where she spent much of her childhood. It would be more than ten years since she had left at 15. I planned to join her there before I returned to Afghanistan.

Meantime as my year contract drew to an end, my boss pressed harder. My students had been well prepared and my class had a 98% pass rate, but he continually found ways to denigrate my work. He told HR I needed his "special counseling". He would call at night and on weekends to try and get me to come to his room. I tried, diplomatically, to schedule his "sessions" in an office setting or after work at the "pit" but he insisted. Finally, I stated openly to him in an email I copied to HR.

"Mr. ____ . I am available for your suggested counseling sessions at the company office or at our place of training, however I do not feel comfortable nor do I think it is appropriate to have these sessions in your barracks bedroom. Could we find a mutually suitable time and place next week?"

He wasn't pleased at all. He summoned the next higher Program manager in Afghanistan to come to HKIA for a meeting with us. The day prior, I'd received a Letter of Agreement (LOA) for the position as Acting Team Lead at NKC. I would have 5 weeks off before I started. I signed the LOA.

My boss hosted the meeting on another section of the base where agency personnel operated. He had us sit down and introduced the Program manager, whom I'd never met even though I'd technically been working for him for about a year. He seemed surprised to see who I was, and my CV was laid before him. He read it over and asked my boss what the issue was. My boss had a speech prepared about how I was undermining his authority by sending an email to HR and by not participating in his counseling sessions. He also added a few hearsay accusations of things I had supposedly said about the team, reported to him by "other females on the team."

I sat and listened. The senior program manager knew we were short staffed, and my credentials and training record was exemplary. He asked my boss what he wanted for the best outcome. My boss answered, "For me to start counseling sessions with her right away". He said I needed to "fit in with their culture" and understand his way of working "so we could work better together." He even threw in maybe I wasn't used to having a black man as a boss, implying I was racist. I continued to be silent.

The Program manager asked me to respond. I replied, speaking slowly.

"I respectfully disagree with your characterization of me. Actually, I will tender my resignation to you. You will be able to recruit someone more in line with your culture."

They were both stunned, I could tell.

"You don't have to resign, Joanne. With some counseling I believe we can work this out."

"No, thank you. Please prepare the necessary paperwork. I will give you one month's notice since I realize you have to run a replacement through CRC and that will take another few weeks."

The Program manager looked at me and saw I was serious. He turned to look at my boss and said, "Ok, give her the paperwork and find a date we need to fly her out. You will need to go through CRC to turn in most of your gear. Sorry to see you go, Joanne."

I knew my boss wouldn't be sorry. I started counting down the days in my head till I could leave his project and the pit. I texted my mates from HTS who were still working on HKIA and we arranged to meet later.

When I returned to the room after dinner, Shala was there. She had her hair color treatment box out. She was searching around for a towel. She looked tired.

"Want me to help you? It will go faster if I apply the color. It's just a root touch up, right?"

"Ok, thanks." We walked down to the ablution block together.

When we pushed the door open, we saw someone already at the row of sinks. The person looked like a man. He looked up at the mirrors and we noticed he had a fair amount of facial hair and a kind of "man bun". He was black, about 5'9" and he/she had on T-shirt and sweatpants. He was flat chested with large shoulders. Definitely a man. He didn't say anything to us but finished washing. He nodded at us and walked out.

"What was that? Was that a guy?"

"Sure looked like it." We both chuckled and Shala put her things on a shelf by the last sink. She put her head down in the sink as I drenched her hair. The color had to set in for about 30 minutes. We sat on the wooden bench by the showers and chatted about our day. I reported what happened with my "counseling", that I had resigned, and I would be leaving in about a month.

"Shala, can you keep a secret for a while."

"Yes, what is it?"

"I already have another job. I signed a contract yesterday. I'll be back in Afghanistan, but not on HKIA. I'll be working at NKC right in the center near the ring road in Kabul."

"Congratulations. I'm happy for you."

"Best thing is I have off for a few weeks. I can be with Sequoia in New Zealand." Shala knew Sequoia from my Skype calls and had spoken to her briefly over the screen a few times.

"I don't know how much longer I'll stay here either. My daughter is getting married next year and I want to save some more money before I leave for good. Wonder if they'll put someone else with me?"

"Maybe not. Not that many females are coming in from what I see. I'm going to the gym early. You're gonna rinse off, right?

"Yeah, don't worry about me. See you later."

My last month on HKIA was hectic. In addition to my training classes, I had more patients from different sectors whom I treated in all sorts of spaces including in one of the changing areas at the gym, behind the DFAC, in other barracks, and in the clinic. By this time, I had a waiver I created for them to sign. I wanted to quantify my treatments for research by having detailed case studies. A faculty member in New Zealand at the New Zealand School of Acupuncture and Traditional Chinese Medicine advised me on the process.

As I was gathering all my gear to turn in to the company representative, my boss came over, double checked my computer and signed off. He introduced me to a woman in our company uniform and said she would be accompanying me to Bagram and making sure I got transport out to Kuwait and then to Ft. Bliss. She was finishing her contract training on KAF. I thought it was strange she should be routed through HKIA, Bagram, and out instead of flying straight out from Kandahar. She was to be my shadow.

When we arrived at Bagram, I was placed with the only EOD (explosive ordnance disposal) female trainer. We shared a room and got to know each other since we were both put on hold for going home. It took over a week to get a transport to Kuwait. Active military always had the first seats.

Turns out my barracks mate had back pain, probably from carrying heavy equipment. We had to carry our heavy duffels up and down stairs. By the time we got to Kuwait she was pale and shaky. I offered to give her a treatment and she said, "Please." We found a back bunk in the general female transit building. It didn't have any sheets, but we were in a hurry.

I did some dry needling on her back and some strengthening points on other parts of her body. She was laying down while I was standing watching the time. Other active duty and contractors (all female) were resting, scrolling or watching us.

Suddenly a large, loud woman trounced over to where we were.

"What's this? Get this shit off my bed!" She was referring to my tall, blonde colleague.

"Is this *your bunk*, lady?" I said coming up closer to her. "It was empty when we came in."

"Yeah, it's mine. I'm going to Afghanistan, bitch. Now, you two, move."

"Whoa," I countered. "Matter of fact we are just coming from a year in Afghanistan and my friend is hurting. Give us 20 minutes to finish this treatment. You can go to the PX while you're waiting. Besides the supply desk doesn't open for another hour."

I gave her my "ol New Yawk" attitude and look. I stood my ground. I motioned for my friend to stay where she was. She still had a lot of needles in her body. Women on the other bunks pretended not to notice this confrontation. I wondered why no one said anything. Were they afraid this would turn into a 'racial incident'?

"You two better be gone by the time I get back. Fuck it." She sauntered out of the area mumbling under her breath. She reminded me of a large puff adder fish.

After I removed the needles, my colleague could walk and felt stronger. We made our way to the supply building to get linens for the bunks we would choose.

"Bet she's a contractor working in supply in Afghanistan, or in the DFAC," I said. "Never mind. Hope we don't have to wait too long for a plane out."

We wouldn't get our higher daily pay rate once we left Bagram. As it turned out we only had to wait about three days before we boarded our "Freedom Bird". It was a welcome flight through Germany and New Hampshire to Texas. I emailed Shala when I arrived safely.

Freedom Bird on the tarmac. Spring 2017
Photo by Laini.

After my time with my daughter in the States and New Zealand, where her book tour was a success, we bid farewell in Auckland. I was happy for Sequoia's accomplishments.

I corresponded with my new company and got a bit of background on the project I'd be working on for Verification,

Testing, Evaluation, Detachment Alpha (VTED) in support of the US Army 4th Psychological Operations Group and the 82nd Airborne. I had to sign a Non-Disclosure Agreement (NDA) and would be "read on" with more details once I arrived in Afghanistan to the NKC base in May 2017.

After a small team from my new company arrived at Bagram, we flew over to HKIA to get our new ID badges and do more paperwork before being flown by helicopter to NKC. We were sent to the transit barracks.

I showed my two company mates the base since it was their first time on HKIA. It was amazing how many people I ran across while walking around just before dinner time. I asked some of my friends if we could hang out in their room until the DFAC opened. They were all former USAF so it worked out well.

One of the Ukrainian doctors saw me and greeted me in Ukrainian. "Dobre Vecher, Joanne" he bellowed.

"What, do you know everybody on this base?" one of my new teammates teased me.

As I walked down the corridor of the co-ed barracks, I saw Shala. She looked much better than a few months earlier.

"Hi, Shala. How are you?"

"Joanne! Wow, what are you doing here?"

"Just in transit. How's things?" We spoke for a few minutes and then we hugged. I promised to text her if I would be back at HKIA for meetings. As it turned out I would only see Shala once more on my way out, in September 2017.

Later, when I was in Iraq in 2018, I received news that Shala had died of a heart attack on HKIA in March 2018. It had come on suddenly, and by the time they got her to the clinic she had passed away.

Her company sent her body and her belongings out by plane. Her family met her Stateside. I sent my condolences to her daughter. Her wedding was planned for the summer. Shala would be there in spirit.

Photo of Shala
in Afghanistan

Shala lived a full life serving both countries she loved, the United States and Afghanistan. She is missed by those who knew and loved her from both nations. It was a privilege to get to know her in the last years of her life.

I think of her often and I treasure the time we had together. She was one of a kind.

# CHAPTER TWELVE

## Sequoia in the Mountains

I'm choosing to share our trip to Nepal in this book because it reflects the various elements of our mother-daughter relationship and Sequoia's singular skills and temperament. From talking with friends of mine who are mothers of daughters about the same age, who face similar challenges with their daughters (especially if they are divorced from the father), I felt it was time to record this part of my life without censoring myself or infringing on Sequoia's privacy.

Some people commented that I didn't write much about my daughter, Sequoia in my first book. That's because for the past ten years, since the death of her brother and father, she didn't want me to speak or write about her or our family. She would get annoyed or angry if she saw I had described her or them in ways she didn't agree with. For the most part, I kept descriptions of our time together, our struggles and our ensemble experiences private, to avoid further pain or misunderstanding.

This chapter literally has us traveling "Between Worlds". We travel to a distant part of Asia, another culture and language to cope with on our journey. We traveled with singular perceptions of what we experienced in Nepal, the people we met, and the tasks we were there to complete. We came together in prayer for our safety, the safety of those with us, and for the sherpa communities and the greater Nepalese society. A country with hospitable, kind and beautiful people under the yoke of a corrupt government and poverty.

To provide a little background, before Marty and I were married, we were already spending most of our free time after work together training for races, mountain hikes and climbs. We were both physically fit because of our work and passion for various sports. Marty was in the USAF Pararescue unit, and I was in the performing arts at that time.

We both loved to swim and to hike in the outdoors. Early in our relationship, Marty introduced me to serious climbing and different forms of skiing.

Marty became a professional mountain guide after he got out of the US Air Force. He accelerated his training and focused on the seven summits, guiding on the highest and most dangerous mountains in the world. He also taught climbing and wilderness skills to small groups or one-on-one clients.

In 1988, my husband, Marty, and I moved to Australia. We were blessed to have a son in Macksville, New South Wales, and later a daughter in Napier, New Zealand. Each child was born with their own unique personalities, in good health with their different talents and tasks in the world. I was overjoyed with the arrival of each of our children.

Our children grew up with climbing gear, seeing both their parents climb and knowing skills for outdoor survival. They also grew up without any television, computers or other tech distractors like video games until Marty and I divorced in 2000. It was an acrimonious divorce.

After that, Marty put all those mod cons in his house as partial babysitters. Our children were exposed fully at ages 11 and 14, which made a significant difference for Sequoia especially, being quite young still at this point. After high school, Denali said he hardly ever watched TV. It was a waste of time, he recognized.

Sequoia was enthralled by TV sitcoms and series. While she lived her last year of high school with my father and his wife, she had her own TV in her bedroom. She became addicted to watching before going to sleep. She also became entranced by social media by the time she was 19. It was hard to dissuade her or point out the adverse effects on spending too much time on screens. Sequoia would have to find this out for herself. Like most of her peer group in the US, she loved taking 'selfies' and posting them on her various social media accounts.

Fortunately, Sequoia still liked to ski, swim and jog. But for a few years while she lived in Houston, Texas she deliberately stayed away from hiking or climbing in the mountains. She concentrated on starting her own business with the help of my father (her grandpa Joe) and living life in a big American city after growing up in rural New Zealand and Australia. I saw her at least once a year while I was working overseas, and we communicated often by phone and email. She wanted to be "totally independent" and moved into her own space by 18 years old, although she had an office right next to my father in Houston. They saw each other at least five times a week. He communicated his observations of her life to me during the time she lived in Houston.

Author climbing in New Zealand 1991. Photo by Marty Schmidt

Sequoia was finding her own way as an adult and hardly saw her brother, Denali, who was studying at university in California.

But that all changed with the sudden death of both Denali and their father, Marty, in July 2013. We lost half our family in one day. Priorities shifted for both of us.

Sequoia told me she wanted to be closer. We each made more effort to include each other in our lives and work. We sat in her office and brainstormed names for each of the imprints for her publishing company, Di Angelo publications. I sent her a ticket in

Author climbing in Yosemite, USA in 1995. Photo by Pepina (lead climber)

2014 to go to Thailand for a 10-day meditation retreat she was interested in, and then onward to Borneo to visit me where I was working in the jungle area of Tebedu, by the Indonesian border. We hiked up in the hills, then down to the city of Kuching, known as the "Cat city". We hired a boat to take us around the harbor. We went to the Orangutan sanctuary and pepper plantation. Sequoia was able to see more of the world. We were both still deeply in grief and to some extent, still in shock in that first year without them.

The next year, Sequoia traveled on her own (against my father and my advice) to Pakistan on her personal mission

Denali and Sequoia in Bear Valley, California.
January 2012.

to try and find the remains of our family. This trip was pivotal for Sequoia. She made a number of life-changing decisions there.

Sequoia compiled her journals into her first book, *Journey of Heart: A Sojourn to K2*. It was successful on a number of levels including receiving an International Book Award and gaining her media attention. She went on a book tour, reading her work in bookstores, REI stores, and other venues. She extended her network and met with people who had known her father and/or her brother.

Sequoia decided to expand her business and move to Los Angeles by herself. She broke off her relationship with her boyfriend. She decided to start climbing seriously both on rock and in higher altitudes. She devoted herself to refining skills she had learned as a child and teenager and began learning new ones, such as ice climbing. It was a way she felt a connection to her father and brother. She said she experienced a closeness with them in spirit when she was in the mountains, or when she was back in places we had gone as a family in New Zealand, California, Colorado, and Australia. Sequoia wore one of her brother's climbing helmets on her first forays into the world's mountains. She had inherited some of his and her father's climbing gear.

Sequoia returned to places we camped and climbed as a family: Yosemite Valley, Mount Rainier, and Mount Aspiring in New Zealand. These were challenging training climbs for the goal she had in mind of climbing in the Himalayan peaks in Nepal.

Sequoia started her push to be in the mountains more in 2016, after her trip to K2 base camp in 2015 and the publication of her first book. Her early training as a child, her natural gifts as an athlete, and her drive to be "near the spirits" of Denali and Marty meant she progressed rapidly.

I was amazed and proud of her new passions, although my mother's heart beat faster as she pursued more dangerous peaks and extreme adventure sports. It wasn't long before she started skydiving, and then learning the most dangerous sport of BASE jumping. To say Sequoia *was not* "risk averse" was an understatement. She welcomed risk in my view, but she said it made her focus and concentrate moment by moment. This was a way to work through grief for her. I did understand on that level. I just couldn't watch all the videos and photos she posted. She was my only living child. I wanted her to live a long, full life.

Sequoia traveled more for work, but we coordinated our schedules to have time together whenever we could in those first few years after their death. In between both of our travels, she and I met in Los Angeles, Texas and in other countries where we created new memories in new places together.

She traveled to many countries over the next few years including Ecuador, Argentina, Russia, Nepal, France, Switzerland, England, Latvia, Singapore, Bulgaria and

Thailand. She was often able to combine her work and travel, since she could work remotely most of the time. Sequoia was becoming a very capable and resourceful young woman. She seemed happier in herself as well.

Sequoia climbing in Yosemite Valley, California in 2016.

Perhaps others who have experienced the sudden death of more than one family member have felt the particular aftereffect of suffering more in the presence of those who remain living, because of the **acute pain of those who are no longer with them.** I don't think either Sequoia or I were fully aware of this phenomenon the first two years after their death. But it was a post trauma reaction that happened when we were alone together.

Sequoia in Ecuador
on Cotopaxi volcano
in the Andes
mountains

I found if we went to a new place together, where there weren't reminders (as much) of who wasn't with us, we could create new experiences and memories in our life without them. It was with this aim in mind I suggested we meet in Nepal during my first break in work in Afghanistan, in November 2016. Sequoia would already be there and we could rendezvous in Kathmandu, a place I had not been before.

Unfortunately, my plane was delayed flying out of Kabul from Hamid Karzai International Airport. In those days I didn't use a spy phone, just a little Nokia flip phone. My sim card from Afghanistan didn't work for Nepal. I couldn't call Sequoia to tell her about the delay. I sent a text which never arrived.

I knew which hotel she would be staying at since it was owned

Sequoia climbing at
Ouray Ice Festival in
Colorado 2016

Sequoia on
the summit of
Mt. Aspiring in New
Zealand 2017

by one of her friends, a sherpa who had summited with different climbers eight times on Everest. He had retired from climbing and started a number of businesses in Nepal. He also had political aspirations. He would accompany us to the Makalu region and show us the place he thought a school was needed. Sequoia was going to help raise funds. I took a taxi to the hotel and left my gear there.

The front desk helped me to locate a kiosk selling sim cards. I finally got through to Sequoia. She sounded irritated. She had been waiting for hours and was worried, but it was almost impossible to explain to someone who has never been in a war/conflict zone the difficulties that can happen in communication and transport. She was with friends at another hotel and said she would be right over. We were not off to the best start.

Sequoia on the
summit of Island
Peak, Mt. Imja Tse,
Nepal 2016

Sequoia arrived with her friend, Tashi Sherpa. He was a smooth businessman. He asked how I liked our room and showed me to his shop for climbing clothes. The jackets were overpriced, but I decided to buy one to support his efforts. Sequoia told me he would take care of the hotel expenses while we were there.

He started talking about how he knew my husband and son. He said he "remembered Denali and what a good climber he was." That's when I knew he was lying—Denali had never climbed in Nepal. The only 8,000-meter peaks he attempted at the end of his short life were in Pakistan in the Karakorum. I kept silent and made a mental note to mention this to Sequoia later.

Sequoia and I in a park in Kathmandu,
Nepal 2016

Sequoia and I had a day to look around Kathmandu together. She enjoyed being my guide. We walked the crowded streets and meandered around the city park looking for monkeys and prayer wheels. We began to relax together in the bustle of the city. We bought Nepalese style T-shirts.

A friend of the Schmidt side of the family joined us. He was about Sequoia's age, but they were just friends. His name was Chris, and he was a police officer in Las Vegas but enjoyed skiing, climbing and photography. He would be making a film of our trip and also be a male companion. This was a surprise. Sequoia hadn't mentioned he would be coming with us. I was polite but a bit miffed.

He'd also recently been injured on the job and was recovering from those injuries. The hikes in the Himalayas would not be terribly difficult. He needed a change and this was his chance to travel, paid for by Sequoia's aunt and uncle, Marty's sister and her husband. They didn't have any children and wanted to be close to Sequoia. This was their way of supporting her and having someone who would "report" back to them. He would be staying with us in the mountain huts. This meant Sequoia and I would not really have time alone. We adapted.

When we arrived at Makalu, we were met by a driver in a jeep-like vehicle. He took our backpacks and we wound up mountain roads to Num. The mountain landscape was stunning. The weather was warm and humid. Chris mounted a GoPro camera on the front of the vehicle. He was constantly taking photos and remarking on the beauty of this region.

At the end of the road, we hoisted our backpacks on our shoulders and hiked into the village we were to stay in, to see the schools Tashi selected. The guest house was very basic. There were no electric lines in the village. The lights were run by generator and the kitchen stoves and refrigerators were run on gas. They used large portable gas bottles like we had when we lived off the grid in Thora valley, Australia.

Our host family prepared food for us at the guest house. We ate lots of lentils and rice called Dal bhat, with greens they called Saag. It was healthy and tasty. We drank copious cups of steaming tea. Sequoia was cheerful once we were at altitude. She played pool at night with the locals at the one recreation place in town. We enjoyed interacting with the many children running about.

We slept in hard bunks in one room. It was chilly at night but we all had cold weather sleeping bags. There was an outhouse, and an outside cold shower. This was how most people in mountain villages lived. Sequoia and I reflected on how differently people in other countries lived. How fortunate we were. We were able to have some private time together in our bunks before we fell asleep.

The two schools were close by. The elementary school was up further in the hills and the high school was near the main courtyard. They were rudimentary wooden buildings

On the way to Makalu Valley, Nepal 2016.
Photo by Chris

with corrugated iron roofs. The classrooms held long wooden tables with wooden benches for the students, large chalkboards, bookshelves, and one teacher's desk and chair. The rooms inside shared the building's outside walls. When it rained it must have been loud against the metal roof with no insulation. I pitied the teachers working in these conditions. They had outhouses and outside sinks.

There were no other buildings I could see. Children played outside and there was one main administrative building near the town center for the principals and secretaries to work. They could walk to either school if needed.

Tashi Sherpas' community was nestled in the mountains, another few hours' hike. It was at an even higher altitude. After two days at 7,000 feet, I was starting to get acclimatized but going up further would wind me. I thought I would give it a try with them the next day. We set out early on foot with our backpacks. Tashi, another sherpa and Sequoia set a brisk pace up the mountain and over the footbridges crossing the rushing mountain river. The air was fresh and thin. After two hours, I started breathing hard. It was quite warm, and it seemed as if my pack were loaded with more weight than I remembered. I asked if we could pause and sit down on the lush grass for a few minutes.

Chris retrieved his camera and took a photo of us in the forest. He also shot a short interview video with me answering his questions about Denali, my work, our life as a family and my thoughts about Nepal on this trip.

Photo of author and Sequoia in Num area of Makalu, Nepal. Photo by Chris.

Village house in the Makalu region. Nepal 2016.
Photo by author.

Sequoia and Tashi Sherpa spoke together for a few moments, then Sequoia came up to me.

"Look, Mum. It's going to be harder climbing from here on up. You're already having trouble keeping up, right? The higher altitude at Tashi's village will make it difficult for you to breathe because you're not used to it. What about you staying near the next village we come to on the way? The other sherpa knows the school teachers there. You could stay in a tent and then return to Num. We'll meet you back there in a few days. That way you can rest. It's your vacation time, right? You don't want to go back to Afghanistan feeling exhausted, do you?"

It was true, I was getting breathless. Tashi's village was still hours walking up into the mountains. I agreed and watched them walk on while the other sherpa who barely spoke English, guided me to a nearby homestead. He went to speak to a young man who was working in a field by a thatched house.

I lay my pack down. It was easier to breathe now. I sat relishing the view and the smells around this simple homestead. The sherpa came back. He said it was "all good to sleep here tonight." We set up a two-person tent and hiked down to where there was a well with a bucket. We washed up and waited for the teachers and their children to return. The young couple who lived on this homestead both taught at the same school. They spoke excellent English. They offered us tea and I spoke with the woman while the sherpa smoked and spoke with her husband. She asked why my daughter and I were up here in Num.

When I explained we were to explore the possibility of building a school with money from a foundation set up to remember my son, Denali, who died with his mountain guide father on K2 in 2013, she paused for a moment.

"Many sherpa fathers and sons die on the mountains. Their only way to make a living is to guide for the mountain teams from other countries. If they had more education, maybe they could do other work. We need better schools but also more educated teachers."

We discussed the Nepalese public school system, the issues with the way schools were cheaply built with no insulation, thin walls and corrugated iron roofs. She confirmed it was very noisy whenever it rained. Teachers with loud voices dominated. You could hear each other since the walls weren't thick. They didn't have enough books. Students had to share and many of the books were frayed or falling apart. They didn't have a school library or a public one. Sometimes the teachers wouldn't get paid for six months due to government corruption or administrators' inept financial handling.

Many children started working at twelve years old. They worked in the fields or as carriers. On our hike I saw a few young, slightly built girls carrying heavy loads with a band over their forehead attached to a large woven basket. Young boys were apprenticed as porters carrying equipment. Older women carried firewood and supplies up and down the hills.

When their children came in for dinner, she asked if I could teach them an English song. I taught them the simple, "If you're happy and you know it, clap your hands..." We all enjoyed singing, laughing together and sharing a meal. They were a kind and generous family living a humble life in this isolated, tranquil part of Num.

The next morning, we packed up the tent and the sherpa insisted on taking one of my packs in addition to his own. I followed him down the mountain to the town of Num. I was always better at down climbing. We made good time back to the guest house.

I walked back to the school at the end of their day. The teacher at the gate greeted me with their traditional palms together and "Namaste". He invited me in and I looked at the schoolhouse and the grounds once more. If we raised enough money to insulate the building, buy books and maybe build a modest library for the school and the community, it would surely benefit these people. This would be a worthy venture for the foundation even if my son, Denali had never been in Nepal. He had hoped to be a teacher, specifically a Waldorf teacher, as well as pursue his career as an artist. He loved children.

My time was spent hiking, looking at the family run shops, and journaling. I was the only tourist I saw. I had time to relax and reflect on my work and life in Afghanistan, in contrast to this peaceful place. Children were happily playing outside until nightfall when it was cooler. I felt genuinely sorry for the children and civilians of Afghanistan, who once knew this type of safety and calm, but who hadn't had peace for decades.

Because there was little electricity, I rose and slept with the sun. There was no internet or WIFI connections in Num. We were mercifully without web contact.

Two days later, Sequoia, Chris and Tashi Sherpa returned. They had a lovely time with Tashi's family and the village people they met. They shared meals together and Sequoia even danced with the women one evening. At one point, they were invited to the Buddhist temple up in the mountains. Prayer silks were bestowed to each of them, and it was an enlivening journey for all of them.

Chris, two sherpas and Sequoia in Buddhist temple,
Nepal, 2016.

When Tashi met us for breakfast the next day he informed us we wouldn't be hiking down and then traveling by truck; instead, he arranged for a helicopter to take one of his relatives who needed hospital care in Kathmandu. We would ride with her back to the capital. Sequoia, Chris and I were to fly in a PC 3. We would have a better view of the Himalayan mountains and valleys. We would also save time. We took one last photo in Num, finished packing and prepared for our departure.

The view from the helicopter window was spectacular. Sequoia and I shared a closer relationship after this trip, and it cheered me to see her smiling and in high spirits. She was joking with us and more affectionate.

Chris, Sequoia, Tashi Sherpa and author in Num, Nepal.
November 2016.

When we returned to the hotel, Sequoia mentioned to me she had samples from her earlier mountain climbs she had to bring back or send back to the USA, but she was worried about customs. Her samples were of defecation from the Himalayan high altitudes. She was part of an organization called *Adventure Scientists*. She was a volunteer researcher. She collected "scat" from the mountains she climbed and sent it back for their "Global Microbe" study. She wasn't worried about carrying these wrapped samples in her luggage leaving Nepal; the worry was entering the USA, or sending it via post.

Since I was working on a military base, HKIA in Afghanistan, and we had military postal service, I offered to take her 'shit samples' back with me. I wasn't worried about my luggage being searched upon arrival in Kabul. I could wrap her package more securely once on base and send it via military post to the lab in the States. She thanked me. We embraced farewell before I left for the Kathmandu airport. I flew back to Afghanistan.

As it turned out, this task proved relatively easy. The whole process went smoothly, and Adventure Scientists confirmed receipt of the samples not long after. I was happy to help her with this project.

Sequoia and I in a helicopter over Makalu, Nepal, 2016.
Photo by Chris.

Sequoia wrote an article about that part of her adventure in Nepal. It was published in April 2017, on the adventurescientists.org site. She titled it, "The Poo is the Glue."

Sequoia's sense of humor does make me laugh, whether she is teasing on the ground or Sequoia is in the mountains. She has always had an impish element to her personality.

The next year Sequoia encouraged me to finish my first volume of poetry. Her company, Di Angelo publications released it for publication in 2017. I titled it *"Kismet"* and she published it under my creative writing name of Jo Patti.

Sequoia and I at a bookstore in Los Angeles, California, USA — 2017.

# CHAPTER THIRTEEN

# Wi Wanyang Wacipi

My maternal grandfather, Salvatore Grasso, came to the United States from Italy after serving in the Italian Navy during World War I. He admired "the Red-ah Man," as he called the first nation people, who were on the American continent before the Europeans came. He never called them 'Indians'.

I was quite afraid of my maternal grandfather. He had a thick Neapolitan, Italian accent, and a deep, booming voice. He also had a bad temper. He was more interested in my four brothers than he was in a little girl. He had three daughters, so his grandsons were his pride and joy.

My grandfather liked to cook. My grandmother didn't. She enjoyed sewing, creating her own patterns, embroidering, and making sure everything was in order. She was much younger than my grandfather. They married when she was 18 and he was 30. She didn't finish high school. She never learned to drive and always deferred to her husband's decisions. My grandma, Rose LaMontagna, was a devoted Catholic woman and a daily prayer warrior. She went to church every day after her daughters were married. She encouraged me to do what she couldn't do in life: travel, learn and be independent. She was kind and humble. I loved her dearly.

My grandfather liked to walk up to the top of Beacon Hill in New Haven, Connecticut, where he and my grandmother lived. He would show me an empty field he said contained "treasures from the Red-ah Man". We would look carefully and occasionally find a flint or part of an arrowhead. When we did dig up an artifact, he would hold it up and remind me to "Always respect the Red-ah Man". I carried

this lesson in my heart and mind for years until I finally met an actual "Red Man".

During the years I attended Georgetown University in Washington, D.C. Activists promoted many civil and human rights causes and opened offices in the District of Columbia, Virginia and Maryland.

By the 1970s, the US government managed reservations and treaties with the Bureau of Indian Affairs. This bureau, incredibly, was directed by non-Native Americans. Corruption was endemic.

A loosely formed organization of urban Native Americans in the 1960s evolved into the national American Indian Movement (AIM). They formed patrols to help reservation and urban 'Indians' be protected against police abuse. They set up native-centric medical clinics and legal clinics, and established an independent school they called Heart of the Earth Survival School.

AIM members participated in Sun Dances, sweat lodges, and other long-hidden ceremonies and 'outlawed' religious practices. AIM was involved in a spiritual battle and movement before, during, and after their occupation of Wounded Knee, South Dakota, in 1973.

AIM members were avowed 'traditionalists'. They cultivated a return to ancestral ceremonies, although Congress would not pass the American Indian Religious Freedom Act until August 1978.

It was only after an action called The Longest Walk, in which hundreds of Natives marched cross-country to Washington, DC., to protest eleven federal bills threatening treaty rights, the conviction of Leonard Peltier, and to press for freedom to practice their religion, that the bills were defeated and President Carter signed the **American Indian Religious Freedom Act** into law.

The FBI was already waging war on AIM, labeling them as 'terrorists'. The US government agencies used every dirty (and illegal) tactic against AIM members and suspected AIM sympathizers in a decades-long fight throughout the United States and native lands in Canada. In the late 1950s, the US set up a program that targeted Native Americans mercilessly. It was/is called COINTELPRO.

COINTELPRO is an acronym for the FBI's Counter Intelligence Program, which was used to monitor, manipulate and disrupt social and political movements in the United States. Dr. Martin Luther King, Jr., the Black Panthers, anti-Vietnam War activists, and the American Indian Movement were among the program's targets. You can do more research into some of the tactics on such Native American veterans as John Trudell, The Poor Bear family, Russell Means, Ramon Roubideaux and many others.

When I was living and working in New York City in the late 1970s and early 1980s, a number of tribal members came to visit and do workshops open to Native and non-Natives. My friend Jo Anderson invited me to speak with a Tsalagi, or Cherokee elder, whose English name was Katherine Leonard. She was holding women-only workshops in New York City for a few months. As I described earlier in this book, I joined her workshop after meeting and speaking with her.

Katherine had us do guided meditations about our mothers and grandmothers and about "being brave".

We would be directed to go to places we feared, such as riding the subways at night in New York City. We went in pairs or in threes. In those years before Rudy Giuliani was mayor, New York City was very dangerous.

Jo moved to Los Angeles to further her career, and soon after I took an offer to work with the San Jose Theatre Company in California. We met up where I was staying in Santa Cruz, California, in 1986. I introduced her to my then boyfriend, Marty Schmidt.

Jo told us of a conference in San Francisco where a number of elders and a few members of AIM would speak. We both had a deep connection to the Native American rights movement and spiritual practices. She didn't have time to go, but thought we would benefit from the experience.

Marty and I went to this conference in 1987. There I had the chance to speak with a few men who were traditionalists. They participated in the Sun Dance (Wi Wanyang Wacipi) in South Dakota. They also warned us against 'commercial Indians'. One of them said to me, "The Red Road is a warrior path. A spiritual path. No one who is a true Medicine man will ever ask you for money. If you are meant to join us, you will be called in your dreams."

Dreams were always important to me. My paternal grandmother talked to me about dreams as messages and placed great importance on them. She impressed upon me since I was a little girl, that I should try and remember them and discover what they had to tell me—or sometimes warn me about in my waking life. My dreams have predicted the most important events of my life, some of which I describe in my first book, *Traveling Off the X*.

A few years later, after Marty and I were married in Australia, and our children were born in Australia and New Zealand, we made a trip back to America to have our children be able to meet some of our family. My father drove out from Texas to California to see us. Marty's family gathered at the Schmidt family cabin in the Sierras for two weeks.

During the second week in America, I had a chance to join a trip organized by the Institute of Noetic Sciences to visit sacred sites in New Mexico and Arizona. These included participating in a sweat lodge (inipi) in Canyon de Chelly.

A Dineh/Navajo family named Yazzie, had their own tour company in Canyon de Chelly. The Noetic Sciences hired them for our tour in Dineh/Navajo lands. We hiked in, then helped set up a sweat lodge and fire. This was to be my first inipi.

The Medicine men who were there spoke to each of us before we entered. After the cleansing and prayers of this sweat lodge, one of the Medicine men looked at a leather necklace I was wearing with my husband's wedding ring. Marty had asked me to wear it along with my own, during my trip away from our family.

The Dineh elder asked if he could feel it, then stated, "Mix blood. Bring tears. Be prepared, sister."

The necklace was made by Marty, whose family was definitely from a different ancestry, culture and religion than my own. He and his family had already brought me many tears in the years I had known them.

It seemed to me this was a warning of more tears to come. His words proved to be too true.

One of the Dineh men heard I had lived in Australia and New Zealand. He asked me about the work I did. I spoke about my work with Link-Up Aboriginal Corporation, trying to find "Stolen Children". He said the "Stolen Children" were still a problem for their people as well. He wondered if I would like to talk to one of his relatives who was kidnapped along with other Navajo children and taken to Christian-run boarding schools. I said I definitely would.

The next day I left the group to go with the Navajo Medicine men to a ranch area outside of Canyon de Chelly to meet with a family. The grandmother invited us into their dwelling and introduced me to the others. She offered us a drink and then asked me about my family, my husband and my children.

After a time one of her sons said he would speak to me. We went behind an out building and spoke privately for about two hours. At the time I didn't know anyone was taking photos. It was supposed to be confidential. His history at the boarding school was painful. I assured him of privacy and took note of the tactics used to kidnap and keep him and others far away from their family, their language,

Speaking with an elder on the Dineh reservation,
Arizona USA 1993

their culture, and their traditions. Only later I found out someone from Noetic Sciences Institute had followed us and taken a photo with a telephoto lens. She sent it to me. I include it here.

The final day of our trip, two of us attended the first day and night of the Ye Bi Chei or Night Chant healing ceremonies at Shiprock, Arizona. We were definitely in the minority there but were treated with curiosity and hospitality. For me, the highlight was the powerful and playful White Mountain Apache Crown dancers. The Night Chants continued for the next week, but I had to return to the Schmidt family in California. The words of the Dineh I met stayed with me in my mind and heart.

\* \* \*

I'd agreed to be part of the Wi Wanyang Wacipi, the Sundance, at Crow Dog's Paradise on the Rosebud reservation in South Dakota. This was at least a four-year commitment beginning the following summer. I prepared by learning songs and prayers in Lakota using cassette tapes and the written language in handouts I was given by Chief Archie Fire Lame Deer and his daughter Josephine when they visited us in rural Australia. I saved part of my salary for the ticket and expenses in 1995-1996. We planned for the family to go over in 1997.

Wi Wanyang Wacipi at Crow Dog's Paradise is held after July 4th holiday every year. It's held on the Rosebud reservation in South Dakota. The first year I went, one of my Aboriginal "sisters" about my age came with me. She was a Ballangarry who danced with the Aboriginal Dance company in Redfern, Sydney. We rented a car in Rapid City since there is basically no public transport to the reservation areas. We came two days early to set up our camp and help on the grounds.

There were checkpoints and Indian security at the entrance to Crow Dogs Paradise. In those days (before 2000) every car and person were checked. They searched for cameras or recording equipment, weapons, drugs and alcohol. These were all strictly forbidden on Sun Dance grounds. In those days some people had cell phones, which were flip phones without cameras. No one smelling of alcohol or pot (Marijuana) was permitted either. I have no photos since none were allowed.

Only Richard Erdoes was given permission to do a number of books with beautiful photos of these ceremonies. He was born in Germany in 1912, and died in New Mexico in 2008. He knew both the Lame Deer and the Crow Dog families. I read most of his books before I visited the reservations in South Dakota in preparation for Sun Dance.

On the Rosebud reservation was where Chief Archie Fire Lame Deer and Leonard Crow Dog held the annual Sun Dance, there was a large banner over the entrance which read, "Crow Dog's Paradise".

Crow Dog's Paradise has a wide expanse of flat, grassy fields, bordered by a river. The days before Wi Wanyang Wacipi started, a tree was chosen, prayed over, cut down and transported to the Sundance grounds. The tree from last year is taken down and the new tree is placed in the center of the Sun Dance arbor. Prayer ties are attached and can be seen blowing in the wind. People go up to the tree and pray. Some place tobacco ties or flesh offerings in their prayer ties. It is a sanctified circle.

We found a spot near the Lame Deer camp. I introduced my friend from the Gumbaynggirr tribe to Chief Archie and his son. She came with me from New South Wales, Australia to South Dakota. Chief Archie wanted to know what kind of dancing she did. He told her, this is a different ceremonial dance she would witness. We prepared to do our first inipi on the Sun Dance grounds.

We gathered sage, fire wood, and cleaned out metal coffee cans for smudging the arbor and dancers with cedar and sage. Then we made our way to the camp kitchen. We sat with some Canadian Cree women I knew. After our meal and conversation, one asked me if I would help her to get more smudge cans ready. My friend was succumbing to jet lag and said she needed to lay down in our tent for a rest.

While we were scooping hot coals into the cans to be ready for smudging, one of the Sun Dance leaders came over and asked us if we could do smudging for the arbor and the dancers for the rest of the ceremony. The next five days. We agreed.

Lakota Sun Dance ground with tree in center of the arbor, South Dakota

We were affectionately called "Cedar boys" since we were the first women to do this task in the arbor. Both of us were grown women with children. Teasing is an integral part of Native American culture which I enjoyed. It's also a way of keeping you humble.

I needed to rise at 4:30 to help prepare the smudging containers, smudge the dancers and Wichasha Wakan before inipis. There were at least four inipis going at one time. It took us a little while to get the rhythm of going back and forth between the inipi lodges and central fires, but soon the Cree woman and I worked together in our own type of dance. We smudged by inhaling the fragrant sage and cedar smoke.

As Chief Archie Fire stated in an interview with Richard Erdoes, in the book *Gift of Power:Chapter Thirteen, The Unexplainable:*

"The English language is useless for talking about sacred things. It lacks subtlety. One cannot express the different shades of concepts with it. Power and Medicine Man, for example, are empty words that, in their raw clumsiness, give only a vague idea of the thoughts behind them. Medicine Man might be a good way to describe a pharmacist, and power might be an acceptable term in the sense of "turn the power on". These words are of no use to me, but what can I put in their place? I am a Wichasha Wakan. You can call me a medicine man, but that won't do. Wichasha Wakan literally means 'holy man', but wakan can be translated in many different ways. It can mean, 'holy', 'sacred', 'mysterious', ' otherworldly' or 'supernatural'. Wakan Tanka, the Creator, literally means 'The Great Mystery'."

When the drumming started, it reverberated throughout Crow Dog's Paradise. I could feel my bare feet on the grass keeping time with the drum beat and later with the heartbeat of the Earth. It was prayer in motion.

The singers from the drum led by John Around Him, called out the traditional songs for the Wi Wanyang Wacipi. Sun dancers came to the fires to check and fill their Chanupa-sacred ceremonial pipes. Many families passed these Chanupa down through generations. We smudged their Chanupa, feather fans, and the human beings preparing.

Native American tribal members were allowed to have Eagle feather fans. I had a hawk feather fan given to me for the ceremonies. Ceremonial fans and pipes should be bestowed, given to you and never just bought. Ceremonial dress, shawls, tobacco and prayer ties should be handmade.

Hawk feather and arrowhead smudging fan

Wi Wanyang Wacipi is not a Pow Wow. A Pow Wow is more a cultural and commercial event.

My children and husband went with me to South Dakota in 1997. Sequoia was chosen as a 'tree girl' and both she and Denali were "Cedar boys" with me at Crow Dog's Paradise. We camped with the Cree women from Canada I met two years earlier, and the Poor Bear family from Pine Ridge. They were part of the larger Crow Dog camp.

Unfortunately, Marty lost his temper on the Sun Dance grounds at Crow Dog's Paradise. We were already having marital difficulties.

One of the Poor Bear family dancers warned him his behavior and anger were not appropriate on sacred grounds and he would be escorted off if he didn't control his temper.

They recognized he was a US Military veteran and a capable man, but he needed to respect the protocols of Crow Dog's Paradise. Outwardly he agreed, but inwardly he blamed me and his anger flared after the ceremonies were over.

I won't go into the years of anguish my family and I went through during and after our divorce. Marty's been dead now for over ten years. However, I will mention this significant betrayal whereby he had me arrested and put in jail.

For months, I was unjustly imprisoned in a number of jails in South Dakota in a large part due to Marty's strategy of "I'll fuck up your life wherever you go".

Photo of me released from Kyle jail in 1997.

I was questioned and roughed up by Sheriff Lineham, and two FBI agents. It was a tortuous time. I was separated from my children. Marty had taken them back to Australia in 1997, while I was being arrested and detained.

At times I was despondent, but my faith in God strengthened. I also met other women who were unjustly imprisoned. Most were also betrayed by someone close to them.

Lakota attorney Ramon Roubideaux took my case. He alerted me after speaking to my husband by phone, that,

"You have an enemy in your camp."

During some of these trials, it was my training and support with Chief Archie Fire Lame Deer and Sun Dancers I knew, that sustained me.

Barbara Means Adams supported me. She invited me to help her mount the first White Buffalo Calf Conference on Lakota Education to be held in Rapid City. She sensed I would be released by the end of the year.

We worked well together. The work enabled me to concentrate on other larger issues than my personal pain.

As it turned out she predicted the outcome correctly. In December 1997, I was finally cleared of all but one misdemeanor charge. I could legally leave to fly back to Australia. I steeled myself inwardly for what I would face when I returned.

Barbara Means Adams on left in glasses, with other
team members for the First White Buffalo Calf
Conference on Lakota Education.
Rapid City, South Dakota 1997.

Marty was already in another relationship with a much
younger Aussie girl. He had been blocking access to our
bank account for me to get funds to pay my Sioux lawyer,
Ramon Roubideaux. Ramon believed in me and defended
me vigorously. He said he could wait for me to pay his fees
once I returned home to New South Wales.

It was clear to me and my father that as soon as I was back
with my children, I needed to start filing for divorce. My
father had been able to visit and stay with my children in
Australia for two weeks during the time I was incarcerated
in South Dakota. He saw the situation with Marty clearly.
He urged me to move back to Texas where he thought
I would have more support.

345

We returned to Texas as a family at the end of 1998. I found a teaching job in Dripping Springs and our children were accepted at the Austin Waldorf School. Marty had promised to change his ways and walk a different path once we returned to the USA. I had given him one more chance. But I doubted he would keep that promise.

I joined a Women's Advocacy group and found a lawyer. My father counseled me to move steadily toward getting a divorce in Texas. Marty was already making our lives difficult again.

After the divorce finally went through, I had an opportunity to be the Principal of the Denver Waldorf School in Colorado the following year. This would mean my children could attend the Denver Waldorf school without my having to pay tuition. I also had a Traditional Chinese Medicine doctor I knew well from Sun Dance in South Dakota. He and his son came over to Australia to teach auricular acupuncture in the Aboriginal community with me in early 1998. He was known as Doc Ron Rosen. He was based in Denver. There was a large community of Sun Dancers based in Colorado. I felt I would have support away from my family in Texas. Marty went back to Alaska, and for a while our life was peaceful in 2000.

As part of our divorce and custody agreement, Marty would have our children for three weeks in the summer. During that time, I would start my Sun Dance commitment with the Menominee in Wisconsin. This time I would be Sun Dancing. I had already been a 'cedar boy' for five years.

In my first year in South Dakota, I met a couple, Norma and Chuck Grignon. She was Lakota and he was Menominee. They Sun Danced at Mary Thunder's Lone Star Sundance with Wichasha Wakan Leonard Crow Dog. They had also danced at Crow Dog's Paradise on Rosebud reservation. Norma grew up on Rosebud reservation and was close with Mary Crow Dog, who later was known as Mary Brave Bird. Over the years I was introduced to and danced with many in the inter-tribal Sun Dance community.

Norma and Chuck came down to Denver to visit and teach me more about Lakota language and Wi Wayang Wacipi. They introduced me to another Sun Dance leader. He was a US Army veteran who had served in Vietnam and who ran inipis in the Denver area. We all sweat together as part of our preparations during the year. We also discussed our dreams and the messages they contained.

For over 10 years I participated in Wi Wanyang Wacipi in South Dakota, Wisconsin and Texas. Five years I was a cedar boy at Crow Dog's Paradise, then I was asked to be a Sundancer with the Menominee on their reservation in Keshena, Wisconsin. I danced for four years in support of the action to save the Wolf River from Sulphur mining.

Before Wi Wayang Wacipi started in the summer of 2000, I stayed with the Grignon family on the reservation. I was "put up on the hill" for Hanbleceya, a rite that is often mistakenly translated as Vision Quest. The correct translation would be "Crying for a Dream." I stayed up fasting and praying for 3 days and 4 nights before they came to bring me down into an inipi to discuss what I had 'seen' and interpret the messages with my Sun dance leaders.

After my first Sun dancing in Keshena with the Menominee, I had glimpses in my dreams and in my consciousness about a terrible event happening in America. We spoke about it in one of the inipis with our Sun Dance leaders after Sun Dance was over. Others also had some of the same images of the tall buildings on fire, people jumping, a huge explosion. I wanted to call out, "Get out of New York!" I had many relatives from my father's side who lived in New York. I felt the world shifting.

I also heard children in many places screaming. They were being 'taken'. I heard the words, "The war is against the children of the world. That is the real terror."

One of the elders spoke calmly about what was to come in the world in the new millennium. He said we were to be the spiritual warriors in the times ahead. He foresaw all sorts of diseases and harm to the human beings, all creatures, and to the waters. He said we were to be the 'protectors'.

"Keep praying and keep to the ways of the Red Road. No drugs, no alcohol, no criminal actions, no violence. Love your families and each other, to keep in good health. Love the truth and love Tunkashila (God)."

My second year of Sun dancing was in the summer of 2001. In May, my son had a nightmare he recounted to me.

"We have to leave America, Mum. We have to leave right away. Something terrible is going to happen here."

Denali always had a strong connection with the spiritual world. I listened to him. I already felt we should leave for other reasons.

I was in the process of making inquiries about moving back to New Zealand. I thought with my divorce and full custody, I would be legally covered returning. Marty only wanted to care for our children for two weeks that summer. Still, it was enough to fulfill my commitment to dance again with the Menominee.

The second year after Sun Dance, the Menominee Sun Dance Leader, Tom, came up to me and asked, "You still want to go back to New Zealand?"

"Yes, I've prayed about it."

He looked at me steadily and then shook his head. I sensed he felt this was not a good decision. He proved to be right.

I said my goodbyes to my Wi Wanyang Wacipi family. We all gave each other the farewell, "See you next year."

My children and I flew out to New Zealand in August 2001. Because of the time zone difference, what most of the world remembers as the tragedy of September 11, 2001, in New York and DC, for us in New Zealand happened on September 12, 2001.

In spite of the horrible custody battle I faced after returning to New Zealand, and the constant attacks by Marty and his friends, I was able to complete my commitment to Sun Dance with the Menominee in Wisconsin for the next two years in the summer of the northern hemisphere, and winter months in the southern hemisphere.

The Sun Dance on the Menominee reservation was a small one compared to those on Lakota reservations. There were only four of us women, to serve the four directions of the four gates of the arbor: North, South, East and West. There were only about twenty to thirty men dancing. Most were from other tribes.

The arbor was filled with Menominee and other supporters watching and praying for the entirety of the Wi Wanyang Wacipi. Drums came from Lakota and Dineh who knew the ceremonial songs. For four years, this was truly a strong, inter-tribal effort. Thereafter, these same lush green grounds serve as a place each summer to hold Menominee ceremonies, feasts and cultural events.

The mining by Exxon company along the Wolf River was stopped before it started. Exxon had originally applied for permits to mine Sulphur and other minerals, back in 1994. In September 2020, the company issued a formal statement:

"We will not pursue further exploration of minerals near the headwaters of the Wolf River."

There is power in prayer. We had acted as 'protectors'.

From 2000 to 2023, as I finish this book, many Sun dancers and Wichasha Wakan (Medicine men and Sun dance leaders) and Native American activists I had the privilege of knowing, have passed on to the spirit world.

These include lekshi (uncle) Chief Archie Fire Lame Deer in 2001, Barbara Means Adams in 2005, Ramon Roubideaux in 2007, Mary Brave Bird in 2013, Mary Elizabeth Thunder in 2017, Leonard Crow Dog in 2021. Doc Ron Rosen died in Denver, Colorado in 2007 and is buried on Rosebud reservation.

Many others, whom I only know by their nicknames or by their faces in the sacred circle over many years, are cherished in our memories. They are no longer living on this Earth but they continue in the spirit world. They were unique and irreplaceable.

Mercifully, some of their children and grandchildren are continuing the ceremonies including Wi Wanyang Wacipi. John Lame Deer and Pedro Crow Dog have learned directly from their grandfathers, grandmothers, fathers and mothers and other elders. They have both Sun danced since they were young children. They are bringing more people to participate in these important spiritual practices.

They and others are keeping these ceremonies alive for the next generations of human beings and for all living creatures. They will pass on reverence for all that God has given us to care for and protect.

Hau Mitakuye Oyasin — All my relations.

Wolakhota — Peace.

Lakota Wichasha Wakan Leonard Crow Dog 1942-2021

# *Photo, Credit*

All photos within the book were either taken by the author or from private collections of photos taken by friends and family, except those noted as being from Facebook pages, Wikipedia free images, or cited from foreign online news sites.

Front and back photos were taken by Denali Schmidt. The front cover is of an expedition on Mount Rainier in the USA. The back cover is from a trip we took in Armenia to Karahenj in 2008.

Please do not copy any of these personal photos without permission from me, the author.

You can contact me via my personal website at: jopattix. com

Thank you,

*Jo Patti Munisteri*
Texoma 2023

# Acknowledgements

Special thanks for reading and editing my manuscript at various stages to: Alan Altimont, Randi Perlman, Rick Swisher, Eric Smith aka Moose, Sean Naylor aka Gretzky, Jonathan Dickinson, Tenyia Lee and Julia at Creative Indie.

# Other Books
# by the
# Same Author

### Non-fiction:

## Traveling Off the X
## by Jo Patti Munisteri

### Poetry:

## CLASH-Poems from Conflict
## Zones by Jo Patti

## Kismet by Jo Patti